AF730450

FAST ACCURATE BIDS

Apparel Decorating Estimating Software

Shop Owner's Manual

Version 3.5

Contents

Introduction

Thank you for choosing Fast Accurate Bids. You now have a tool to help you streamline the apparel decorating bid process.

The concept behind Fast Accurate Bids is to offer you, the shop owner, both control and simplicity in the bid creation process. Our goal is to enable everyone in your business to confidently create customer bids based on your business's pricing policies.

This manual explains the settings and features available for customizing Fast Accurate Bids for your particular business. It also provides suggestions on best business practices around the bid process.

Fast Accurate Bids comes with several pricing profiles that specify the charges, markups, and other variable settings for the program. For example, three of the pricing profiles that come with the software are **1 Lowest Price Bid**, **3 Middle Price Bid**, and **5 Highest Price Bid**. The screen printing settings for the built-in pricing are based on an industry-wide survey of pricing. The embroidery settings are based on recommendations by industry expert, Deborah Jones.

If you're new to the apparel decoration industry and uncertain about what to charge, you can start immediately by using the built-in pricing profiles. For example, if you're a screen printer, consider using **3 Middle Price Bid** for most jobs, one of the lower price pricing profiles for highly competitive bids, and one of the higher price pricing profiles when working on jobs for which customers are willing to pay more to get exactly what they need.

If you're a seasoned apparel decoration business owner and want to customize the pricing for your particular business, the only thing you need to do is save the built-in pricing profiles you find useful to a different name and then make the changes you want. (The built-in pricing profiles are Read-Only files that get updated and replaced each time that Fast Accurate Bids issues a new release.)

Creating your own set of pricing profiles will allow you to generate bids that accurately reflect your current business model and pricing. This means that the bids you create will be accurate, consistent, and repeatable.

In addition to this manual, Fast Accurate Bids provides a *User Manual* that explains how to create the bids and a *Price List Creator Manual* that explains how to use the Fast Accurate Bids Price List Creator. The goal is to make the bid process so easy and reliable that you will feel secure allowing even the most inexperienced person on your staff to create bids for your company.

Setting up Fast Accurate Bids

The three essential tasks for setting up Fast Accurate Bids for your business are:

1. **Review, and if needed, create additional Pricing Profiles for your business**
   A pricing profile is a saved list of the charges, markups, discounts, and other settings that are used as the variable values for this program. Fast Accurate Bids comes with a number of built-in pricing profiles. You can use the built-in pricing profiles for creating bids and for creating your own customized pricing profiles. Working with the pricing profiles is described in detail in the chapter in this manual called Managing pricing profiles.
2. **Update the supplier connectors with the current prices**
   The term "supplier connectors" refers to the software programs within Fast Accurate Bids that allow you to download the pricing files for the suppliers you work with. Before you start using the software to create actual customer bids, be sure to update each of your supplier connectors so that you have current pricing information. How to perform this task is described in detail in the section in this manual called Updating supplier pricing files.
3. **Customize the Microsoft Word template**
   The Microsoft Word template that is shipped with Fast Accurate Bids allows you to efficiently incorporate the calculated bid information into a finished document that can be sent to your customer. How to open the template and edit it to display your company's logo and the standard text that you routinely use is described in detail in the chapter in this manual called Adapting the Microsoft Word Template.

In addition to the three essential tasks mentioned above, this manual also describes how to:

- Use Password Protection. This lets you control access to the Profile Settings Page and the Pricing Analysis Page so that this information cannot be viewed or changed by anyone who does not know the password.
- Turn on and off the display of the item cost. This lets you hide the display of your item costs on the Choose Item Page and the Design and Pricing Page. Being able to see item costs is useful when doing bids in private, but when generating a bid with the customer present, this feature lets you to keep your costs confidential.
- Set up a Supplier Connector update reminder. This lets you set a display reminder for keeping your supplier pricing files current.
- Use the Pricing Analysis Page. The Fast Accurate Bids Pricing Analysis Page provides detailed data on the pricing calculations for each line item. It shows a listing of the customer information, decorations, charges, and discounts for the line item displayed in the Design and Pricing Page.
- Set up price lists. Fast Accurate Bids allows you to create pricelists with pre-defined prices based on the number of items, and number of sides, etc.

Understanding and using pricing profiles

Fast Accurate Bids comes with a set of built-in pricing profiles. The screen printing settings for the built-in pricing are based on an industry-wide survey of pricing. The embroidery settings are based on recommendations by industry expert, Deborah Jones.

You can also create your own additional pricing profiles to meet your business needs. Fast Accurate Bids lets you create as many pricing profiles as you want.

A pricing profile is a file that contains the charges, markups, discounts, and other settings that are used as the variable values for deriving a bid's pricing. This information includes the following:

- All the settings and values on the Fast Accurate Bids Profile Settings Page
- The name in the **Prepared By** field on the Design and Pricing page

The pricing profiles operate on a line item basis. In other words, as you add line items to your bid, you can switch from one pricing profile to another. For example, if you charge a higher markup on low-cost items versus ones that cost more, you can enter the line items for the lower cost items using one pricing profile and select a different pricing profile for the higher cost items. If this is the case, consider setting up pricing profiles with names like **0 to $4 Items**, **$4.01 to $7 Items**, **$7.01 to $11 Items**, and the like.

You can save a pricing profile to any alpha-numeric name and also use a dollar sign ($) in the name. You cannot use other special characters like the ampersand (&) or semicolon (;) in pricing profile names.

An important thing to keep in mind is that the pricing profiles are central to creating accurate, consistent bids for your customers. It's important that you understand how to use them, that you assign names to them that clearly identify when to use them, and that you educate your staff on what they are so that everyone in your business who creates bids will clearly understand how to use them.

The pricing profiles that start with **1 - Lowest Price Bid** and go to **5 - Highest Price Bid** are intended for screen printing bids. For embroidery bids, the built-in pricing profiles start with **Emb 1-Head 1 Lower** and go to **Emb 6-Head Higher**.

Important: When using the built-in pricing profiles, keep in mind that they do not take into account considerations that may be important to your particular business. Fast Accurate Bids offers the built-in pricing profiles as a starting point and highly recommends that you take the time to create a set of custom pricing profiles for your business.

Managing pricing profiles

The Profile Settings Page is where you manage Fast Accurate Bids pricing profiles. If you click the drop-down list in the Profiles Management Settings area of the Profile Settings Page, you can see all the pricing profiles that have been set up for your installation of Fast Accurate Bids. These are simply versions of the settings shown on the Setting Page that have been saved under a descriptive name so that you can use them when creating bids. Fast Accurate Bids lets you create as many pricing profiles as you want.

To access the Profile Settings Page, click the **Show Settings** button at the bottom of the Design and Pricing Page. If you don't see this button, it means that a password has been set up for your version of Fast Accurate Bids and you have not entered the password for the program. For more information see Using password protection.

The screen shot below shows the Profile Settings Page for the pricing profile **3 Middle Price Bid.** To see other pricing profiles, click the drop-down arrow to the right of the Choose Profile field and select them from the list that appears. You can only view one pricing profile at a time.

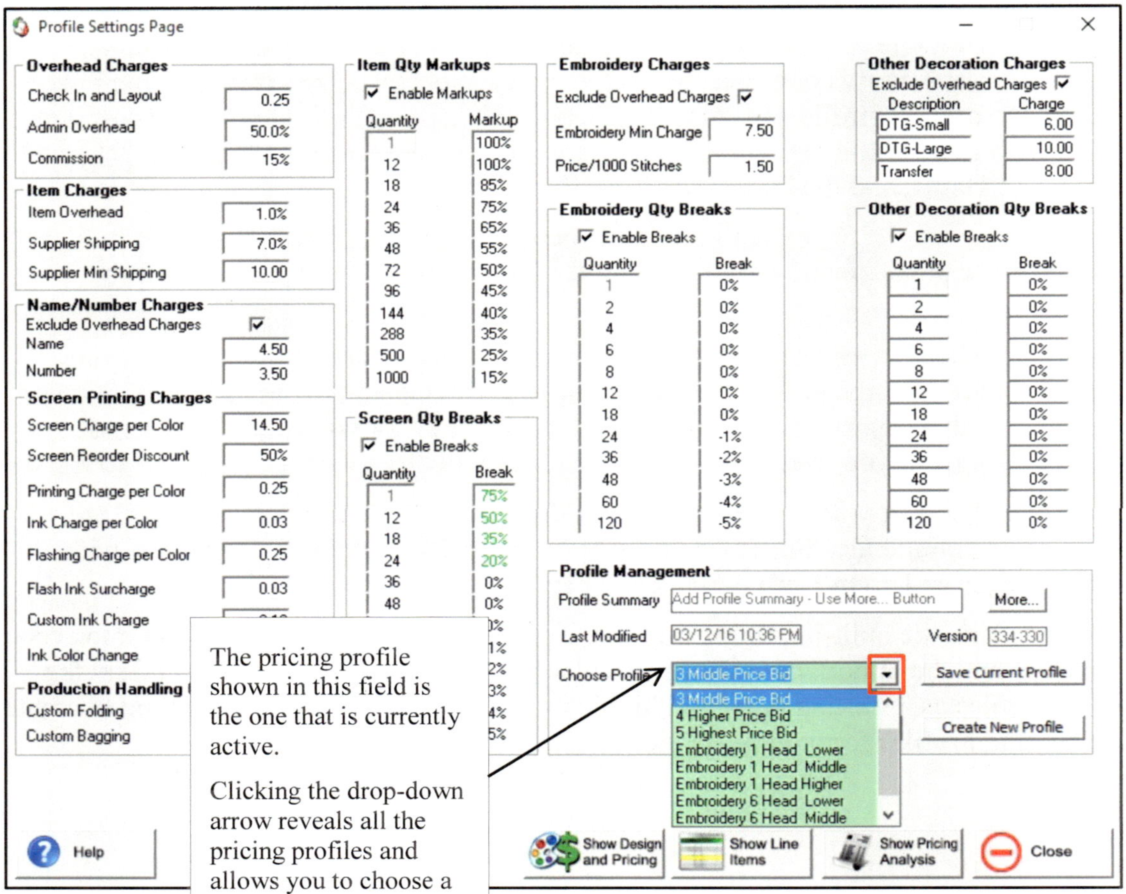

The pricing profile shown in this field is the one that is currently active.

Clicking the drop-down arrow reveals all the pricing profiles and allows you to choose a different one.

Things to note

- You can hide the Profile Settings Page if you do not want everyone in your company to have access to this sensitive data. For more information, see Using password protection.
- The values you see on the Profile Settings Page always relate to the currently selected pricing profile.
- The built-in pricing profiles are read-only files. You can use them without changes for creating bids. You can also save them to a different name and make any changes to them that you choose.
- To edit a pricing profile, select the pricing profile from the drop-down list in the Profile Management Settings area of the Profile Settings Page, click in the field you want to change, and enter the new value. The new value is set as soon as you tab out of the field, and the settings are saved when you click **Save Profile**, change to a different pricing profile, or close this page.
- You do not need to close out of Fast Accurate Bids for changes to a pricing profile to take effect. The new setting will be used for the current line item (if there is one on the Design and Pricing Page), and for all subsequent line items in the current and future bids.
- If you want the Fast Accurate Bids software to ignore any of the settings for any particular pricing profile field, highlight the value in the field and set it to 0 (zero).
- In preparation for doing a general price increase for your business or any other task that involves making a significant number of changes to your pricing profiles, consider setting up a folder such as **/My Documents/ Fast Accurate Bids/ Pricing Profiles/Backup** and copying a set of your profiles to that directory.
- Keep in mind that whenever you install a Fast Accurate Bids update, the install program replaces all the built-in pricing profiles to assure that you have the benefit of our most recent pricing survey. It does not, however, remove pricing profiles that you create.
- To keep your list of pricing profiles manageable, consider deleting any of the pricing profiles that you are not interested in using.

The Summary and Details for the pricing profiles

You can edit the pricing profile field **Profile Summary** and the associated details by clicking the **More** button.

You may enter up to 40 characters for the summary and up to 255 characters for the details. Consider using this feature for such purposes as explaining the intended use for a profile, specifying when to use (or not use) the profile, or specifying the differences between the current profile and another profile.

The field **Profile Summary** can be used to augment the profile's name with additional information or to enter the first several words of the profile details when you need more than 255 characters for your comments. Alternately, you can simply enter the profile name in this field.

When you click the **Save and Close** button, Fast Accurate Bids saves the text in the dialog box and also saves the pricing profile.

There is also a **More** button (which is view-only enabled), on the Design and Pricing page.

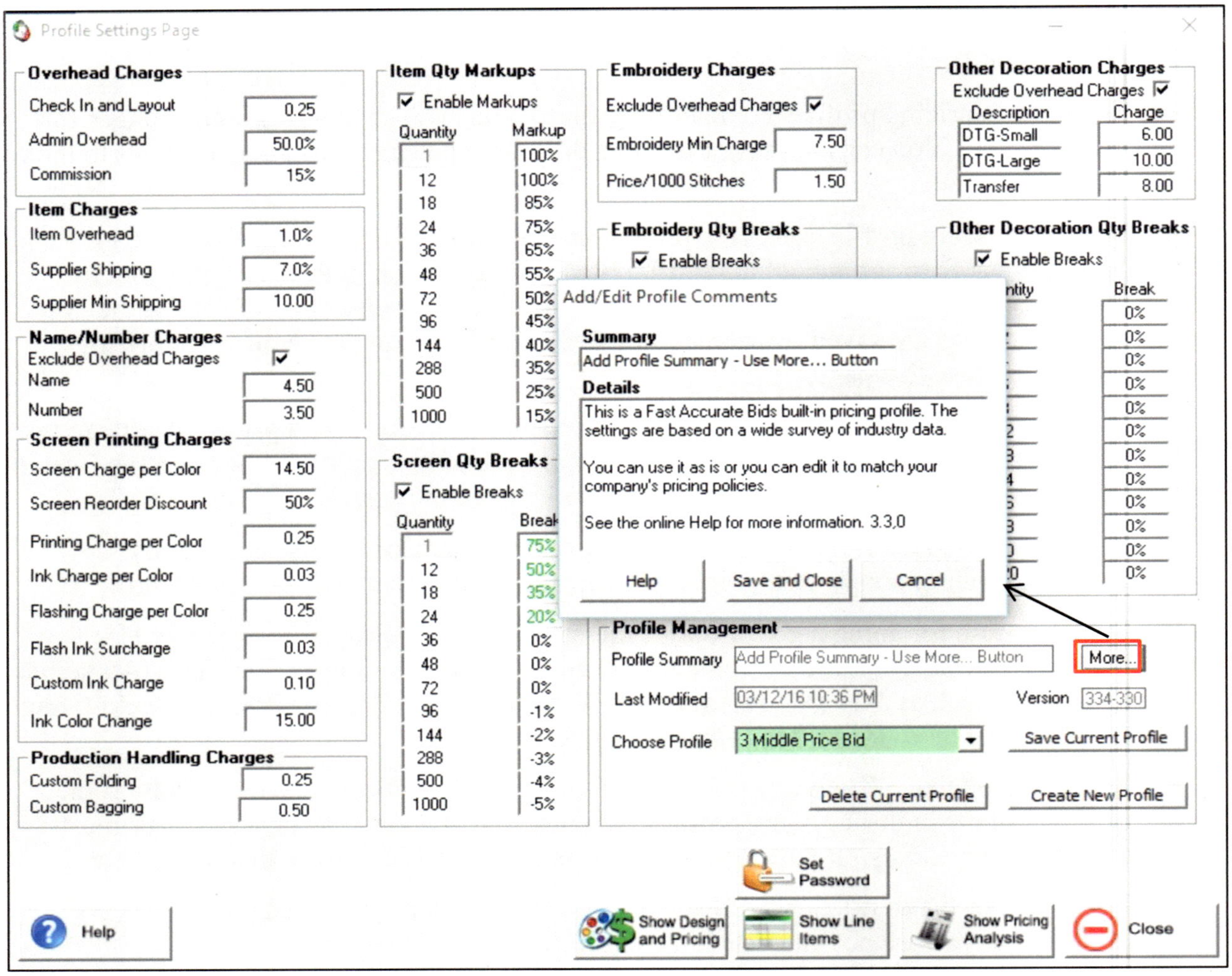

Fields on the Profile Settings Page

The following sections discuss the fields on the Profile Settings Page grouped by the way that they appear on the Settings Page.

Overhead Charges

The Overhead Charges settings are located top left of the Profile Settings Page.

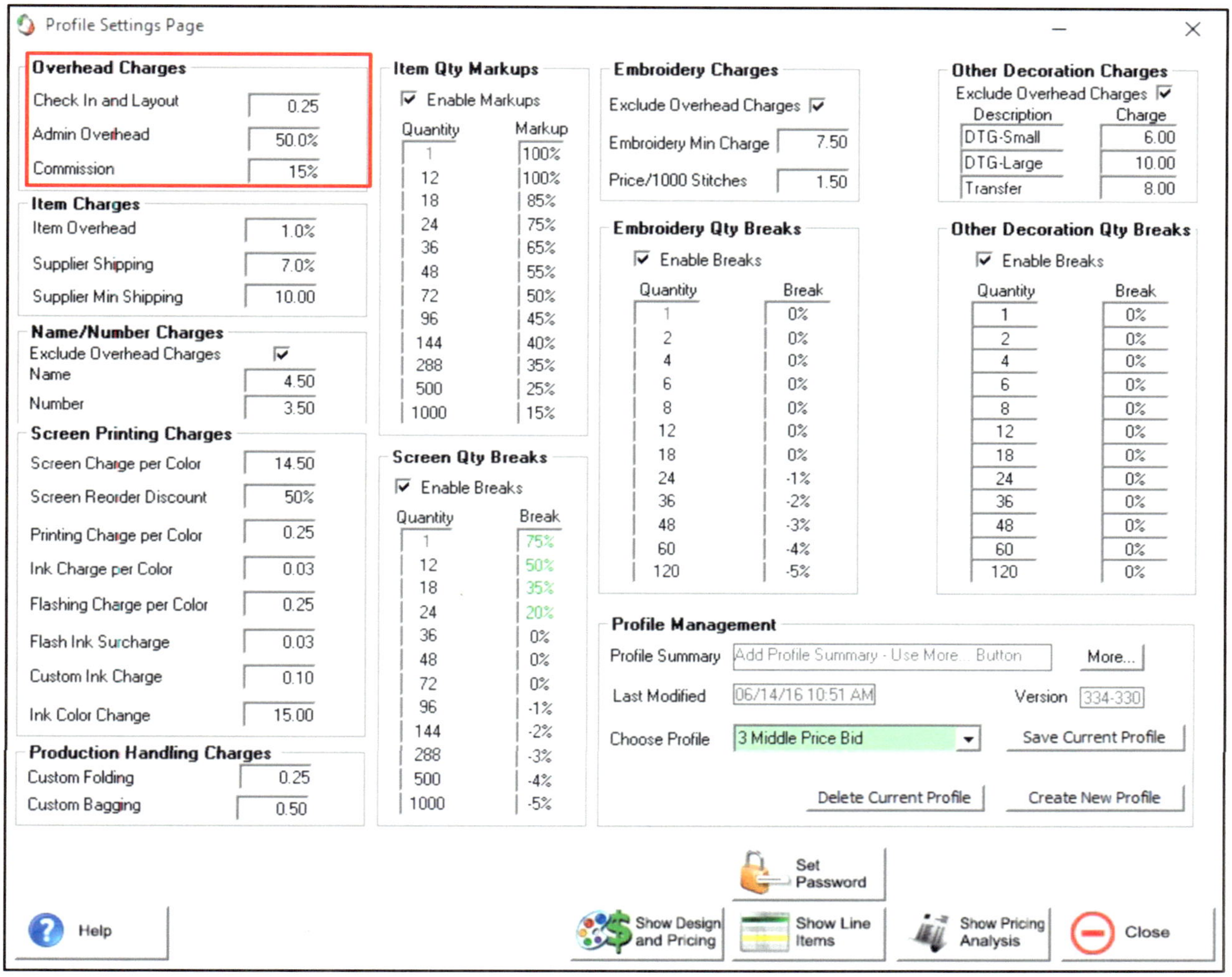

Check In/Layout

The **Check In/Layout** charge is the charge per item that you want used to cover the time it takes to unpack items, count them, stack them for decoration, lay them out again after decoration, recount them, and repack them for delivery.

This charge gets applied for decoration area (**Front**, **Back**, **Left**, or **Right**) you select on the Design and Pricing page.

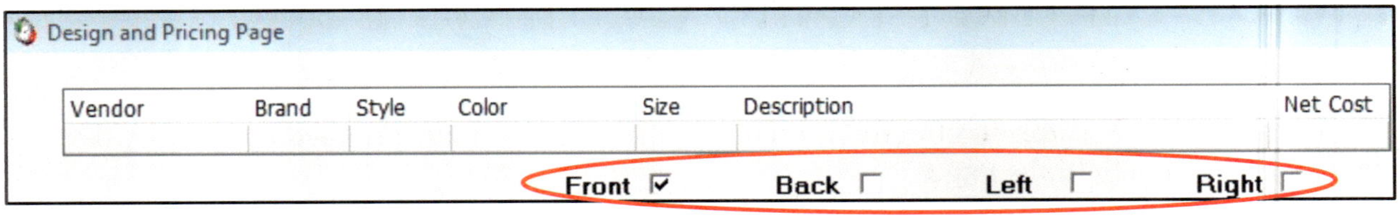

To determine how much this charge should be for your business, divide your target hourly rate by 60 to get your target revenue per minute. Next, multiply your target revenue per minute by your estimated number of minutes it takes to handle each item.

The way to get a reasonably accurate estimate for your business on the number of minutes it takes to handle each item is to do some time studies on several small, medium, and large projects.

Here's how to go about his process,

1. When a shipment for a project comes in, time how long it takes to unbox it, count and stack the items for decoration.
2. After the decoration process is done, time how long it takes to restack, recount, and rebox the items for pickup (or shipment) to the customer.
3. If the project requires decorating more than one side of the item, time how long it takes to re-stack the items for the additional decoration tasks.
4. Add these times together and divide by the number of items for the order.

Once you have an estimated time for handling each item that you have confidence in, multiply that number by your target revenue rate per minute. For example, suppose your time studies show that it takes you just less than one minute each to check in, layout, and rebox an item, and your target revenue rate per minute for your business is $0.66 ($40 per hour / 60 minutes). If this is the case then, consider setting **Check In/Layout** to **0.66**.

Important: Don't forget to do your time study on several small, medium, and large projects so that you get a reliable estimate that represents more than just one size of order.

Administrative Overhead

Admin Overhead is the percentage to be charged to cover overhead costs such as your production margin, rent, non-billable staff time, equipment costs, utility bills, and insurance. When used, administrative overhead is calculated on the price of the item just prior to applying the commission percentage.

Admin Overhead is not applied on the net cost for items. The settings for the Item Qty Markup are used to calculate the markup on items.

Commission

Commission is the commission percentage to be paid to your sales representative for the sale. The commission amount is calculated using the customer price times the commission percentage.

Note: If you do not have a sales person for your business, consider putting in a percent for commission anyway to pay yourself for the time it takes you to interact with your customers in answering their questions and preparing their bids. Also, if you add a sales person to your staff sometime in the future, you will not have to raise your prices to cover the portion of the work that the new person takes on for your business.

Item Charges

The item charges are located at the upper-left of the Settings Page, just below the Production Handling Charges.

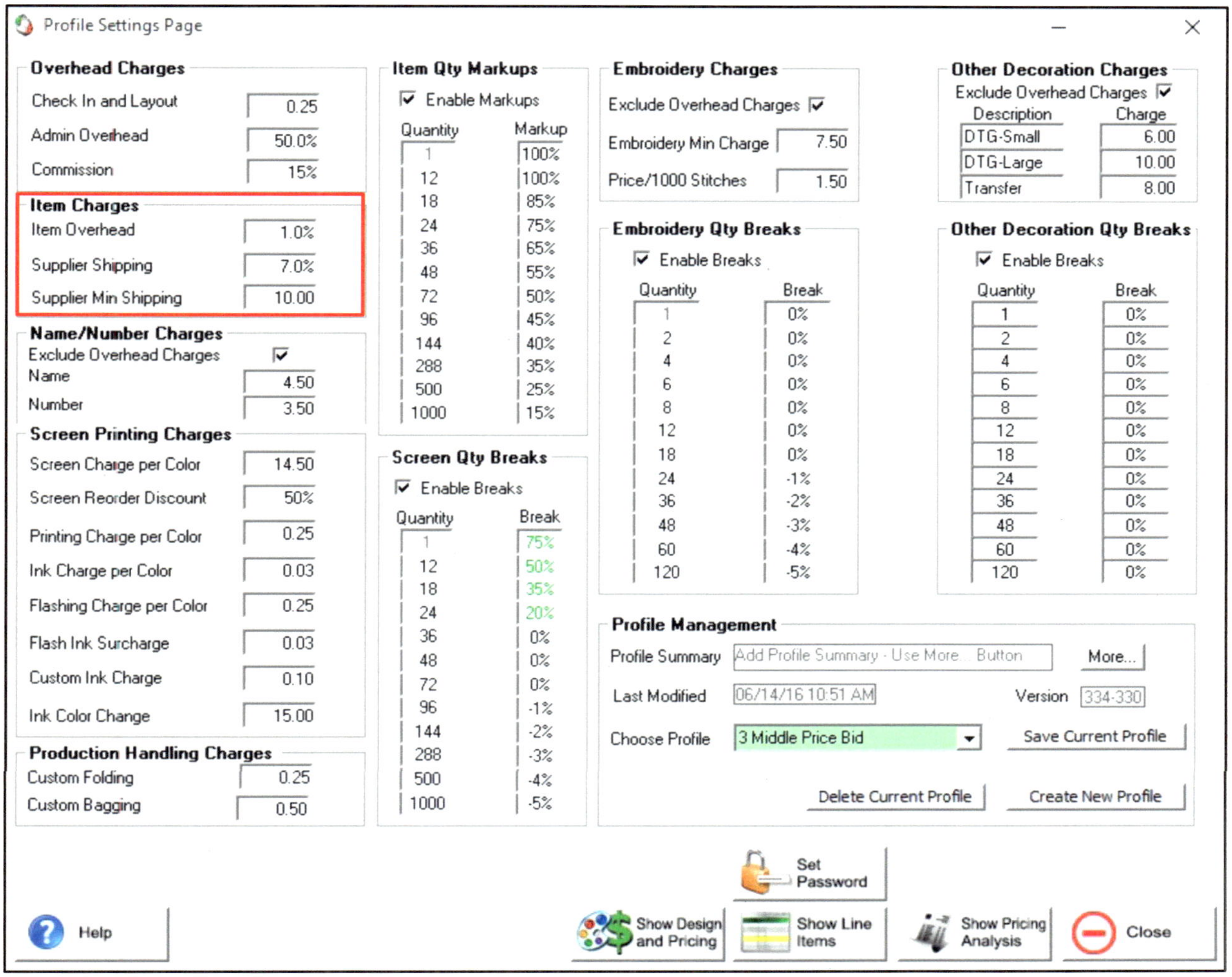

Item Overhead

Item Overhead is the percentage to be charged to cover costs for things such as misprints, defective items, labor, time for ordering items, etc. The item overhead is applied before the Item Qty Markup has been applied to the item cost.

Note: The cost for shipping items from your wholesale supplier to your shop is handled separately from **Item Overhead**. Fast Accurate Bids provides the fields **Wholesaler Shipping Percent** and **Wholesaler Min Shipping** to capture these costs.

Supplier Shipping Percent and Supplier Min Shipping

The **Supplier Shipping** and **Supplier Min Shipping** fields are used to calculate the estimated cost of shipping items from your wholesale supplier to your shop for decoration.

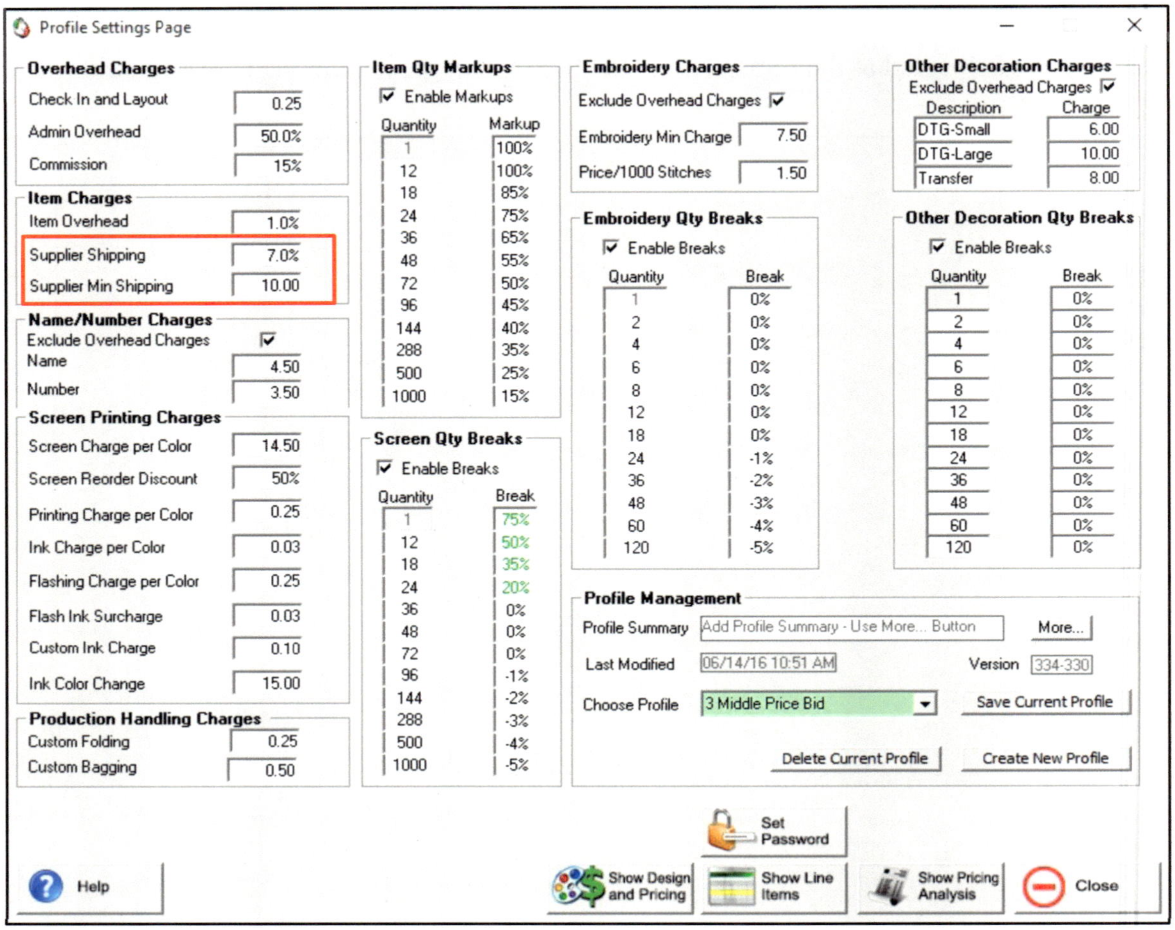

The fields for adding the shipping charge to the bid are located at the right side of the Design and Pricing Page in the Shipping from Supplier area.

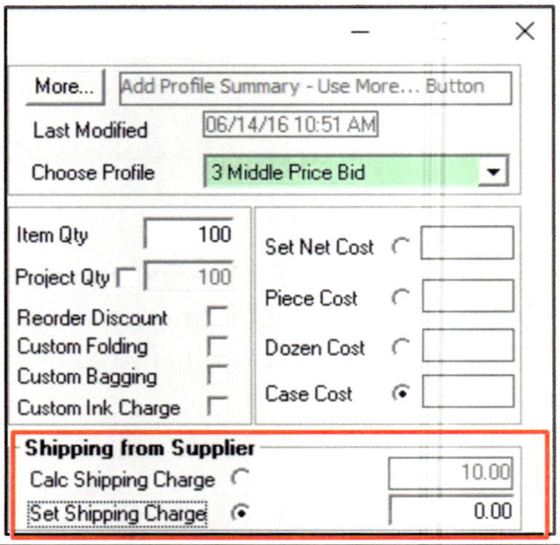

The calculated shipping charge is the higher of either:

Supplier Shipping x Item Cost x Item Qty

Or the amount specified in the field **Supplier Min Shipping**.

Because wholesale suppliers often waive the shipping costs on orders over a specified amount, the Design and Pricing Page sets the shipping charge to $0.00 and lets you choose whether you want to enter a different amount for the shipping or choose the calculated shipping charge.

This allows you to adjust the shipping charges for a bid on a line item basis.

Name/Number Charges

The Name and Number Charges are located at the left of the Profile Settings Page just below the Item Charges. In addition to the fields for **Name** and **Number** is a check box labeled **Exclude Overhead Charges**.

Select the **Exclude Overhead Charges** check box if you want the name and number charges to be the exact amount charged to the customer. In other words, if you have already factored in your check in and layout charge, administrative overhead, and commission on your name and number charges, then selecting this check box lets you continue to use the amount for your name and number charges that you are accustomed to using.

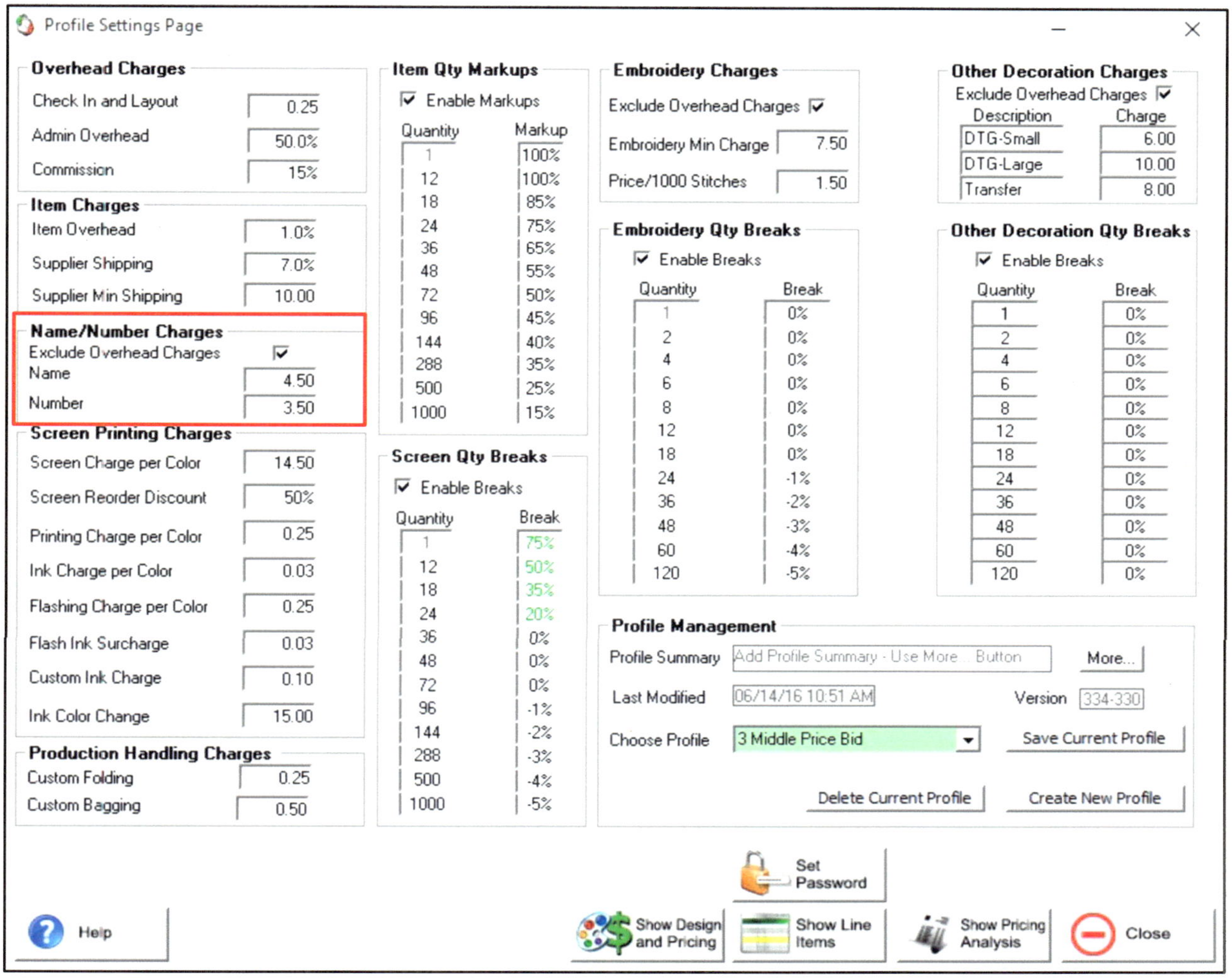

Name is the amount you charge for putting individual names (or any individual words) on shirts. For example, putting individual employee's names and their job titles on shirts.

Number is the amount you charge for putting individual numbers on shirts. For example, putting individual player's numbers on athletic shirts.

The check boxes for choosing **Name** and **Number** on the on the Design and Pricing Page are at the bottom of the area for the apparel decoration choices in the section labeled **Other Charges**.

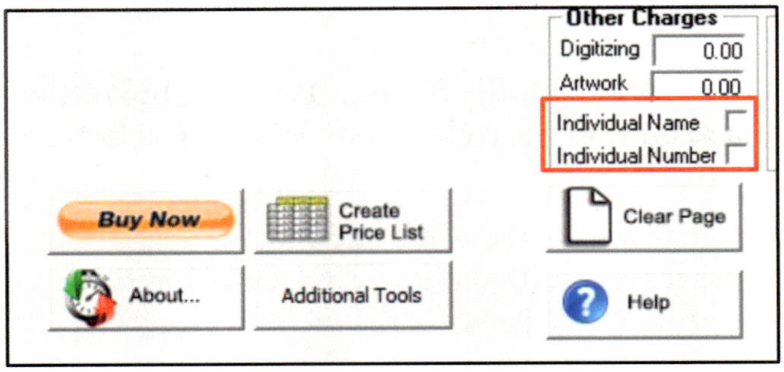

Screen Printing Charges

The Screen Printing settings are located at the left of the Profile Settings Page, just below the Name and Number Charges area. These are the settings specifically related to screen printing calculations.

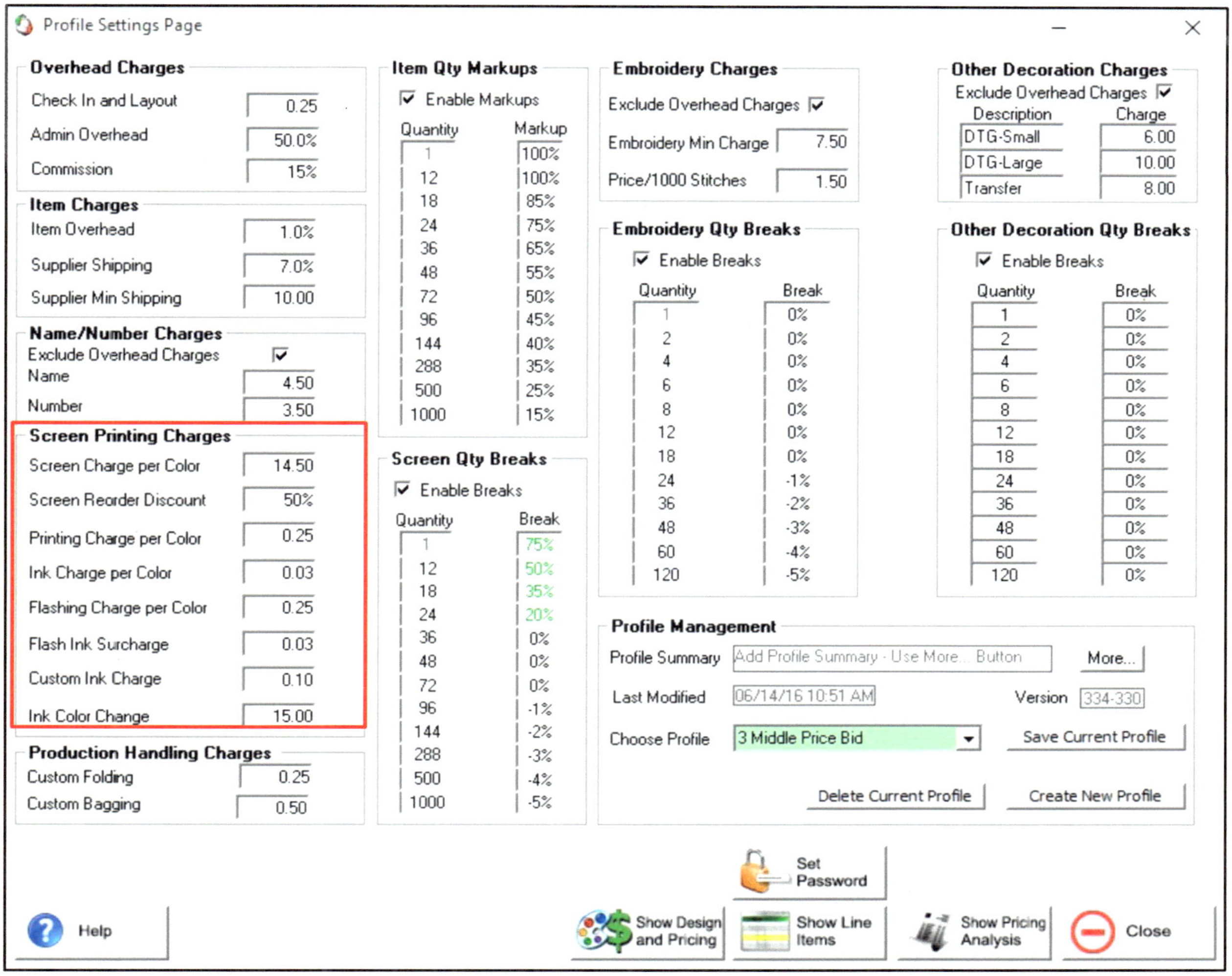

Screen Charge/Color

Screen Charge/Color is the cost for each screen for printing. This is intended to cover the labor and materials associated with the use of the screen.

The labor portion consists of the cost of coating the screen, burning the image on it, taping it for printing, registering it on the press, and after the job is done, reclaiming it for future work.

The materials portion consists of a percentage of the cost screen itself (which is based on the number of times the screen can be used), the emulsion for the screen, the film for the image, the tape, and the chemicals.

Screen Reorder Discount

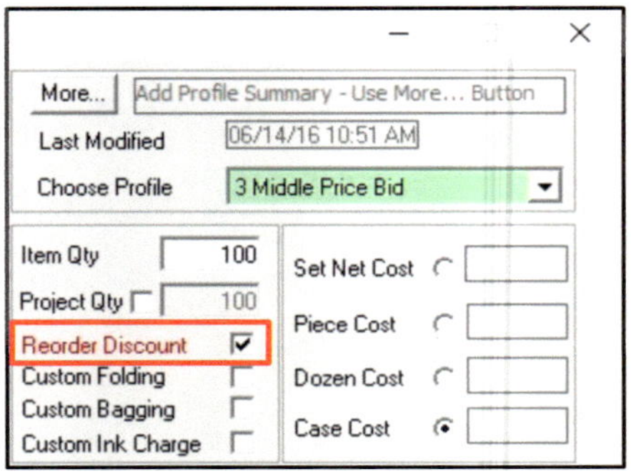

The **Screen Reorder Discount** enables you to give your customers a price break on reorders, since much of the work to prepare the screens for the job has already been done.

When the **Reorder Discount** check box on the Design and Pricing Page is selected, the Screen Reorder Discount is applied to the amount in the **Screen Charge/Color** field.

The **Reorder Discount** check box stays selected until you unselect it. For this reason, Fast Accurate Bids turns the label for the check box red to enhance its visibility whenever the discount is being applied.

Note: The Pricing Analysis Page allows you to see the screen printing discounts used for an item both as a percentage and as a dollar amount. It also shows the discount for a reorder. For more information on the Pricing Analysis Page, see Using the Pricing Analysis Page.

Printing Charge/Color

Printing Charge/Color is the amount for labor to print one color on one item.

Ink Charge/Color

Ink Charge/Color is the amount for ink to print one color on one item.

Flash Charge/Color

Flash Charge/Color is the additional amount to cover the time it takes to flash cure ink during printing. There are fields on the Design and Pricing Page for selecting the number of flashes for each of the sides of the item.

Ink Surcharge for Flashing

Ink Surcharge for Flashing is a markup percentage that is applied to the **Ink Charge/Color** field to calculate the ink cost for items that are flashed.

Custom Ink Charge/Color

Custom Ink Charge/Color is the additional amount for screen printing on items that require an additive for the ink. This charge is intended to recover the cost of ink that must be discarded after printing the job; for example, printing on nylon items, or discharge printing. The value for this setting is multiplied by the sum of the quantities in the Design and Pricing Page fields **Colors** and the **Item Qty** to determine the amount to charge.

The check box for charging for the use of custom ink is located at the upper-right of the Design and Pricing page in the same area that is used for entering the item quantity.

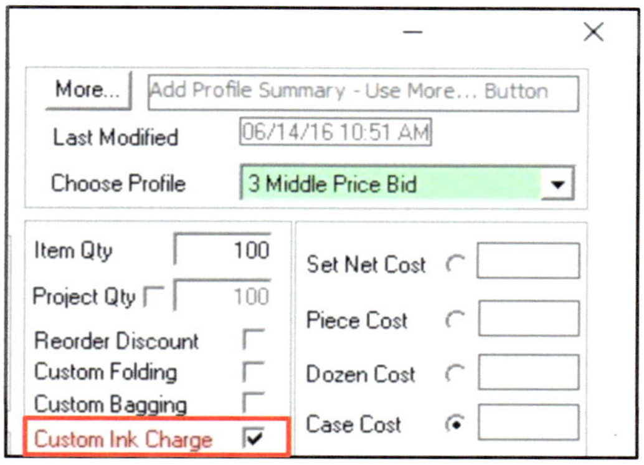

The **Custom Ink Charge/Color** field will stay selected until you unselect it. For this reason, Fast Accurate Bids turns the label for the check box red to enhance its visibility whenever the charge is being applied.

Note: The Pricing Analysis Page allows you to see the custom ink charge used for an item both as a percentage and as a dollar amount. For more information on the Pricing Analysis Page, see Using the Pricing Analysis Page.

Ink Color Change

The Ink Color Change field lets you add a charge if the job requires changing the ink color for one or more screens. This charge is intended to cover the time it takes to clean the ink from a screen and re-ink it.

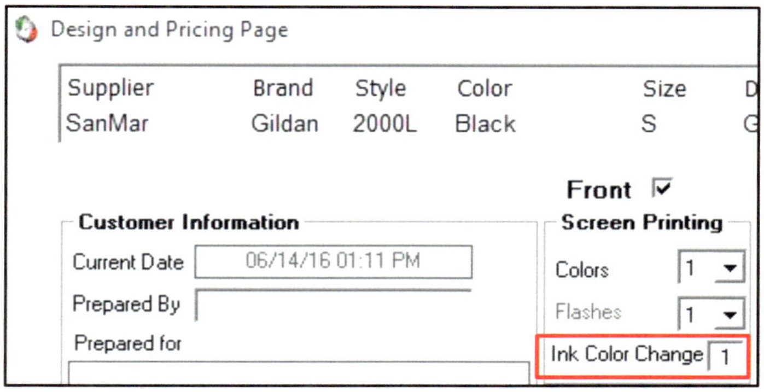

The field on the Design and Pricing Page for selecting an ink color change charge is located with the screen printing decoration choices.

Production Handling Charges

The production handling charge settings are located at the lower-left of the Profiles Setting Page.

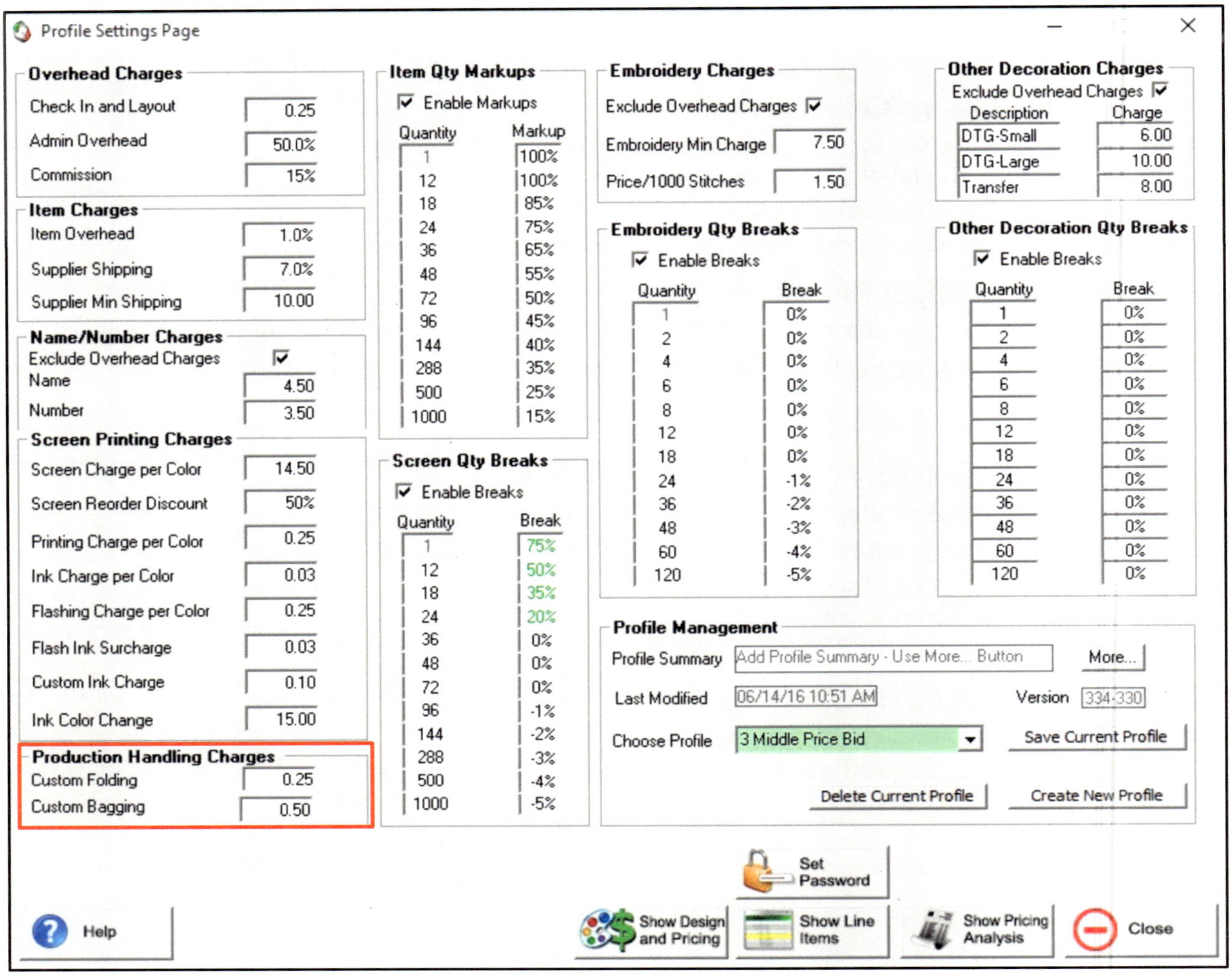

Custom Folding

The **Custom Folding** charge allows you to add an additional charge for individually folding the printed items for the customer. This charge can also be used for other special handling of garments requested by the customer.

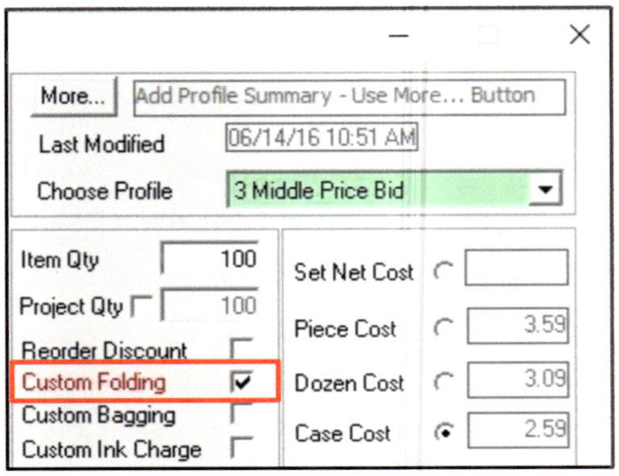

The check box for choosing **Custom Folding** on the Design and Pricing Page is located at the upper-right of the page in the same area as the fields for quantity.

The **Custom Folding** field will stay selected until you unselect it. For this reason, Fast Accurate Bids turns the label for the check box red to enhance its visibility whenever the charge is being applied.

Custom Bagging

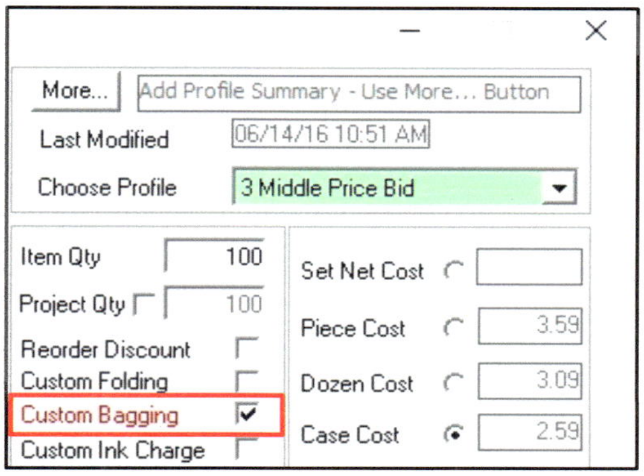

The **Custom Bagging** charge allows you to add a charge for the individually bagging finished items. The amount you enter in this field is intended to cover both your cost of the bag and the time it takes to fold, insert, and seal the item in the bag.

The check box for choosing **Custom Bagging** on the Design and Pricing Page is located at the upper-right of the page in the same area as the fields for quantity.

The **Custom Bagging** field will stay selected until you unselect it. For this reason, Fast Accurate Bids turns the label for the check box red to enhance its visibility whenever the charge is being applied.

Item quantity markups

The table for **Item Qty Markups** lets you to specify markup percentages on your cost for the items ordered. This table is located at the top of the Profile Settings Page, just to the right of the Overhead Charges area.

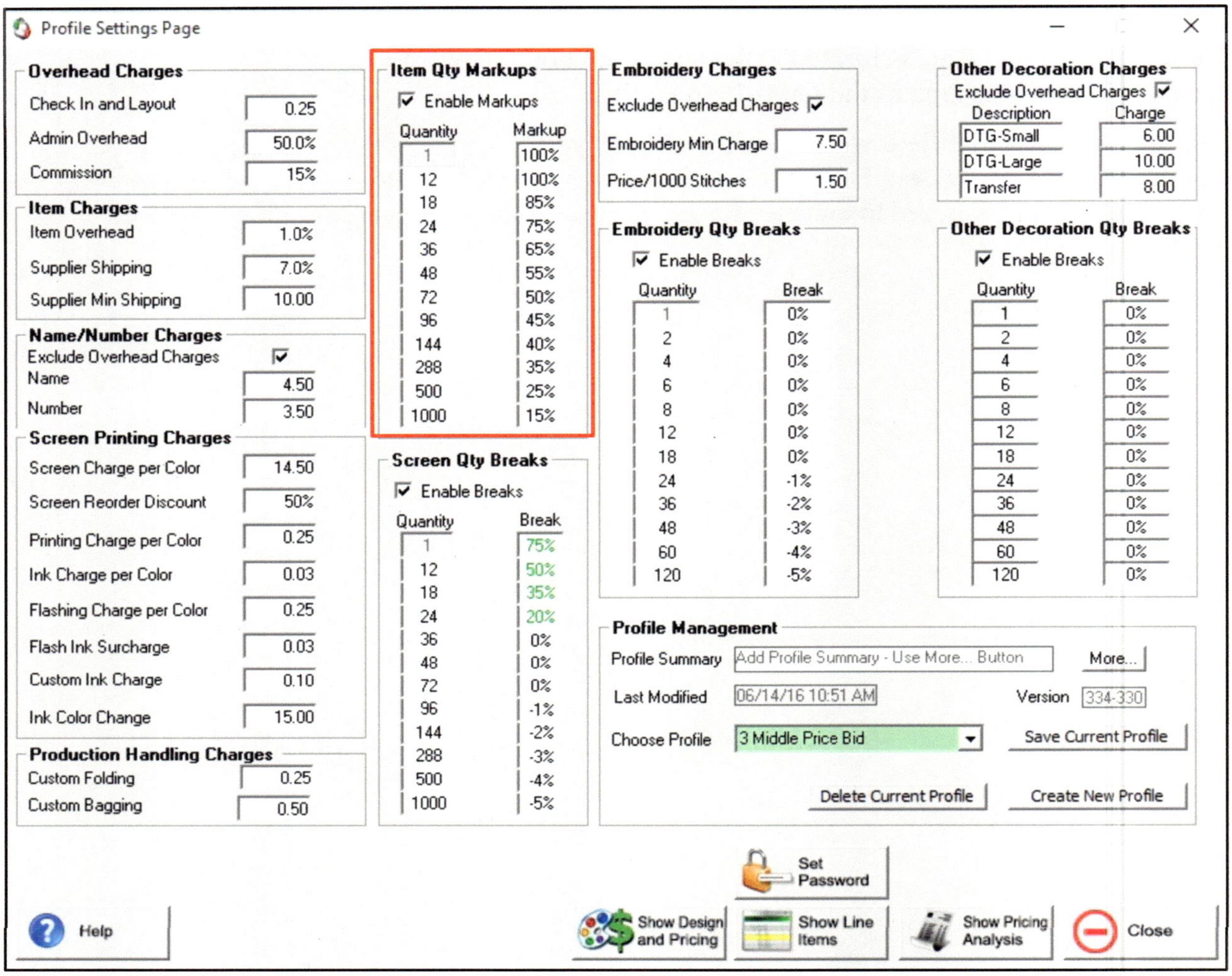

The Item Qty Markups table lets you set up price breaks as the quantity of items increases. If you turn off this feature (by unselecting the **Enable Markups** check box at the top of this area), no markup is applied to your cost for the apparel items.

The Pricing Analysis Page allows you to see the markup used for an item both as a percentage and as a dollar amount. For more information on the Pricing Analysis Page, see Using the Pricing Analysis Page.

Note: If you want to use the same markup on items regardless of the quantity sold, set the first entry on the Item Quantity Markups table to a number larger than you ever print in any one job (e.g., 99999) and set the markup to the percentage markup you want applied.

Screen quantity breaks

The **Screen Printing Qty Breaks** table, which is just to the right of the Screen Printing Charges section, lets you to set price breaks to provide a discount on the printing charges as the quantity increases.

The printing quantity break is applied to the fields **Check In/Layout, Custom Folding, Custom Bagging, Screen Charge/Color, Printing Charge/Color, Ink Charge/Color, Flash Curing Charge/Color, Flash Ink Markup, Ink Color Change,** and **Custom Ink Charge**.

The percentages in the **Screen Qty Breaks** fields are calculated pricing adjustments and can be either a surcharge or a discount. Entering a positive number is treated as a surcharge on printing. This feature can be useful for small print quantities to ensure that you are adequately compensated for the time it takes to set up the job, since it takes as long to set up a job for 12 items as it does for 100.

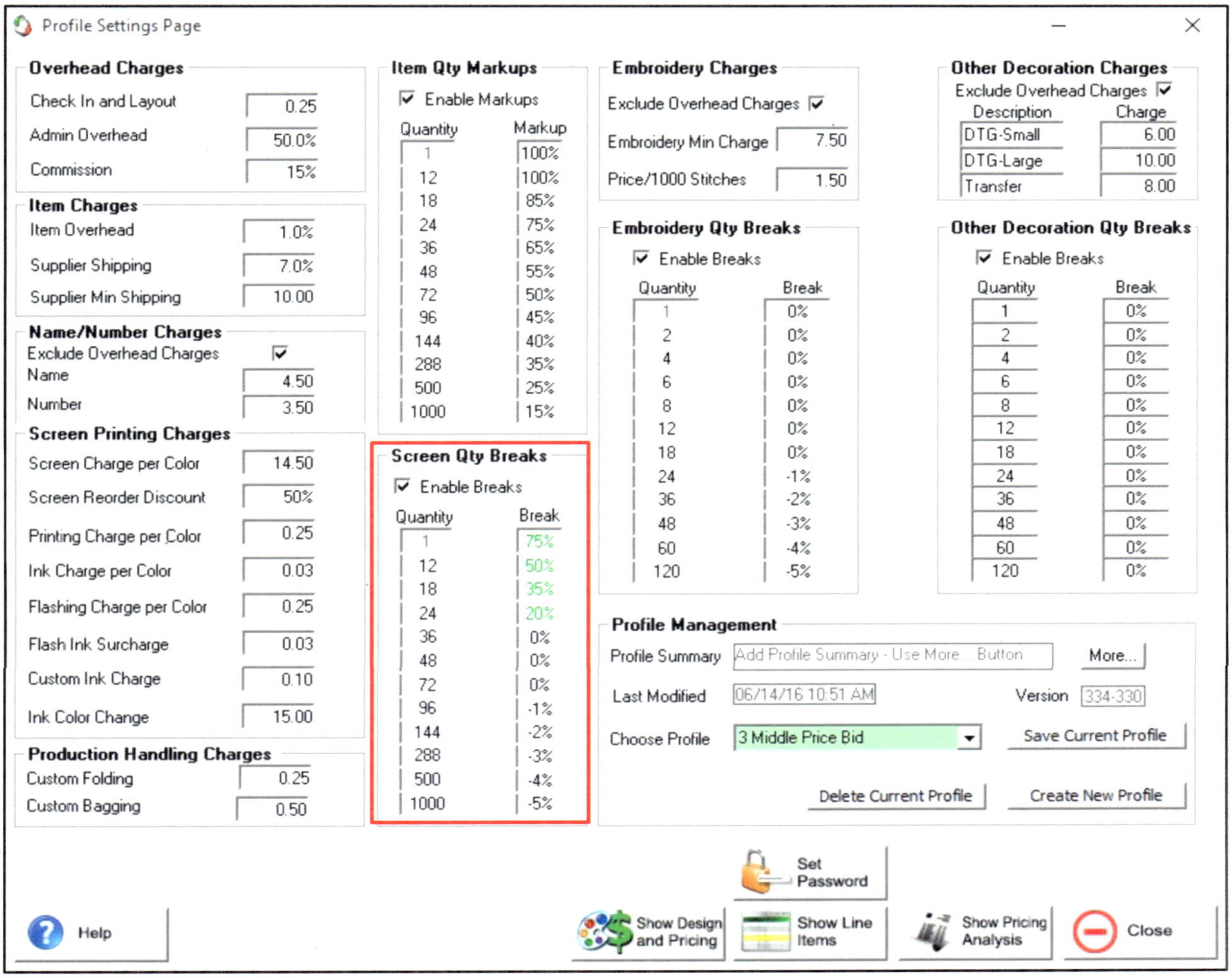

Things to Note

- Enter a positive amount to set up a surcharge. For example, if you have a 36 item minimum but occasionally make exceptions, consider entering a surcharge for screen printing quantities of less than 36 items.
- Positive percentages in the screen printing breaks table are displayed in green to indicate that they will be treated as a surcharge.
- Enter a negative amount to set up a discount. For example, enter **-5** to give a 5% discount.
- If you turn off this feature (by unselecting the **Enable Breaks** check box at the top of this area), no price breaks are applied to the screen printing charges, regardless of the quantity for the line item.

Embroidery charges

Fast Accurate Bids provides settings for a **Minimum Charge** and **Price/1000 Stitches** for embroidery charges. It also provides a check box labeled **Exclude Overhead Charges**.

Select the **Exclude Overhead Charges** check box if you want the embroidery decoration charges to be the exact amount charged the customer. In other words, if you have already factored in your check in and layout charge, administrative overhead, and commission on your embroidery decoration charges, then selecting this check box lets you continue to use the amount for your embroidery charges that you are accustomed to using.

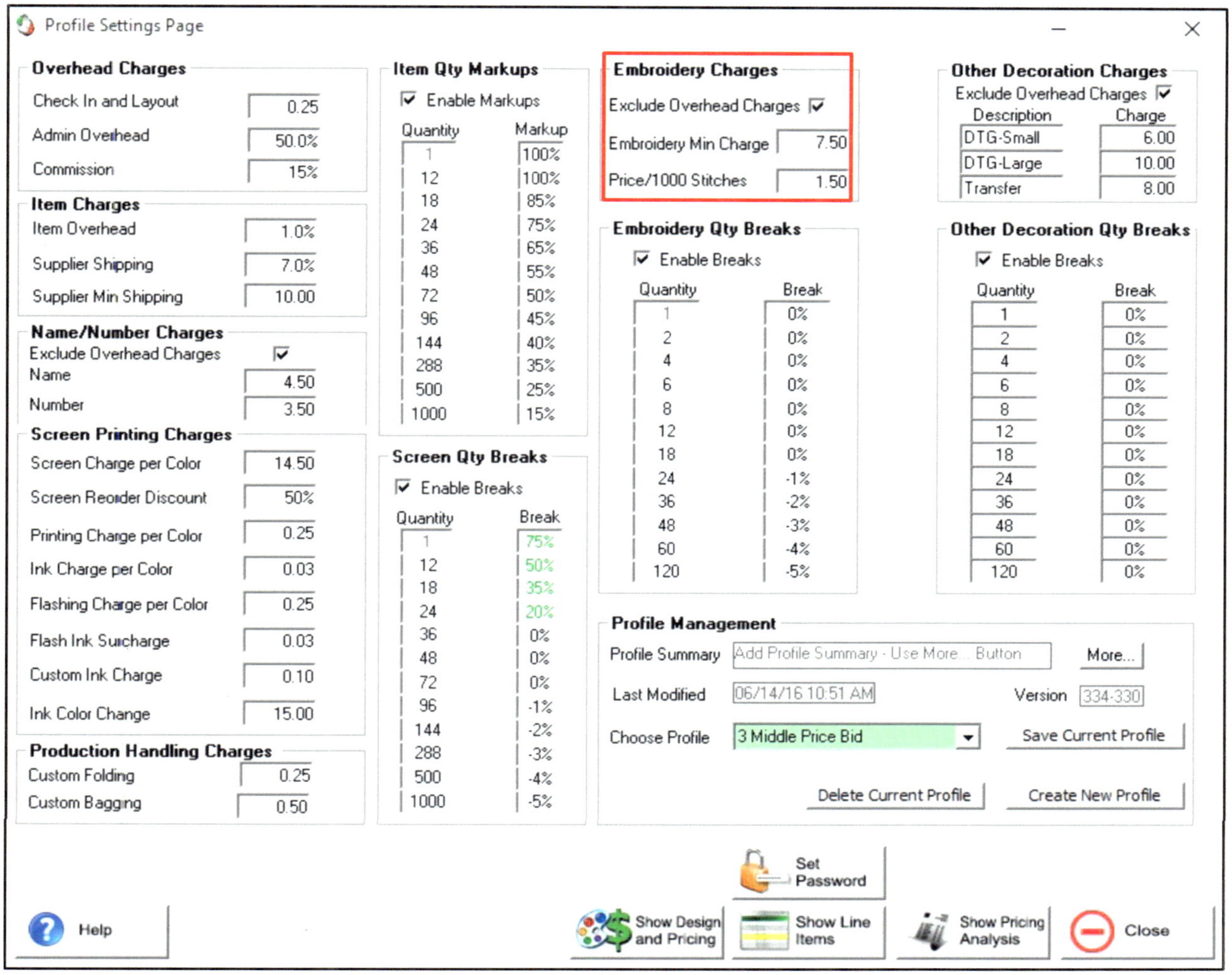

The screen shot below shows how the pricing choices for embroidery are shown on the Design and Pricing Page. **Custom Price** button on the Design and Pricing Page lets you access a dialog box to enter a price on-the-fly when creating bids.

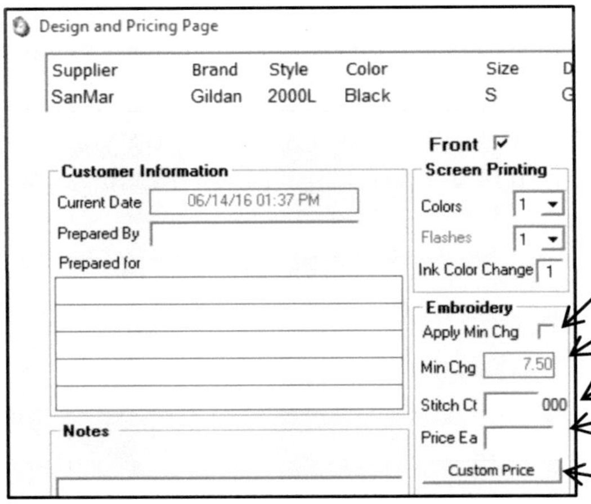

Lets you to apply the minimum charge for embroidery.

Displays the minimum charge amount set on the Settings Page.

Lets you enter the number of stitches to get a calculated charge.

Displays the amount that will be charged for the embroidery. This field can also be used to directly enter an embroidery charge.

Lets you access a dialog box to enter a custom price for the embroidery.

Things to Note

- When creating bids, if you use more than one of the embroidery pricing methods, the amount charged will be based on the method last used. For example, if you enter a custom price (using the Embroidery Custom Price dialog box) and then enter a stitch count, the charge will be based on the stitch count without regard to the amount you entered using the Embroidery Custom Price dialog box.
- The number in the field **Stitch Ct** represents the number of thousands of stitches in the embroidery. For example, enter **12** for a design with 12,000 stitches. This field does not accept decimal values. So, for a design with 11,585 stitches, it is up to you whether you choose to round up to **12** (for 12,000 stitches) or round down to **11** (for 11,000 stitches).
- The behavior of the **Exclude Overhead Charges** check box does not affect the embroidery quantity breaks. The calculation for embroidery quantity breaks remains the same regardless of whether the Exclude Overhead Charges check box is selected or not.

Embroidery quantity breaks

The **Embroidery Qty Breaks** table, which is just below the Embroidery Charges area of the Profile Settings Page, lets you to set price breaks to provide a discount on the embroidery charges as the quantity increases.

The percentages in the **Embroidery Qty Breaks** fields are calculated pricing adjustments and can be either a surcharge or a discount. Entering a positive number is treated as a surcharge on embroidery. This feature can be useful for small quantities to ensure that you are adequately compensated for the time it takes to set up the job.

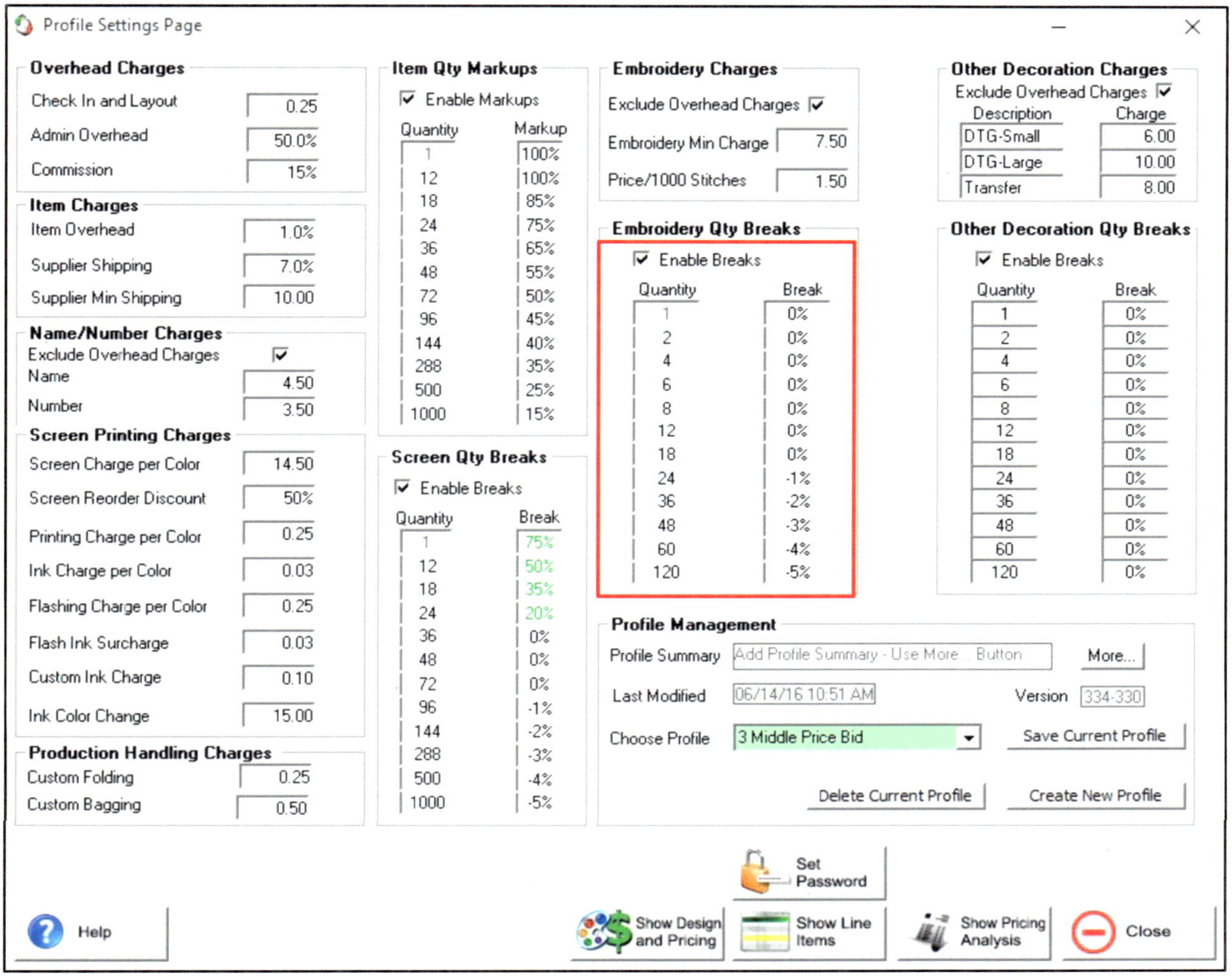

Things to Note

- Enter a positive amount to provide a surcharge. For example, if you have a 6 item minimum but occasionally make exceptions, consider entering a surcharge for quantities of less than 6 items.
- Positive percentages in the embroidery quantity breaks table are displayed in green to indicate that they will be treated as a surcharge.

- Enter a negative amount to provide a discount. For example, enter **-4** to give a 4% discount.
- If you turn off this feature (by unselecting the **Enable Breaks** check box at the top of this area), no price breaks are applied to the screen printing charges, regardless of the quantity for the line item.

Other Decoration Charges

The Other Decoration Charges settings are at the top-right of the Profile Settings Page. You may specify whatever decoration techniques you want for Other Decoration Charges.

The Other Decorations choices for the built-in pricing profiles are **DTG – Small**, **DTG – Large**, and **Transfer**.

There is also a check box labeled **Exclude Overhead Charges**.

Select the **Exclude Overhead Charges** check box if you want the other decoration charges to be the exact amount charged the customer. In other words, if you have already factored in your check in and layout charge, administrative overhead, and commission on your other decoration charges, then selecting this check box lets you continue to use the amount for your other decoration charges that you are accustomed to using.

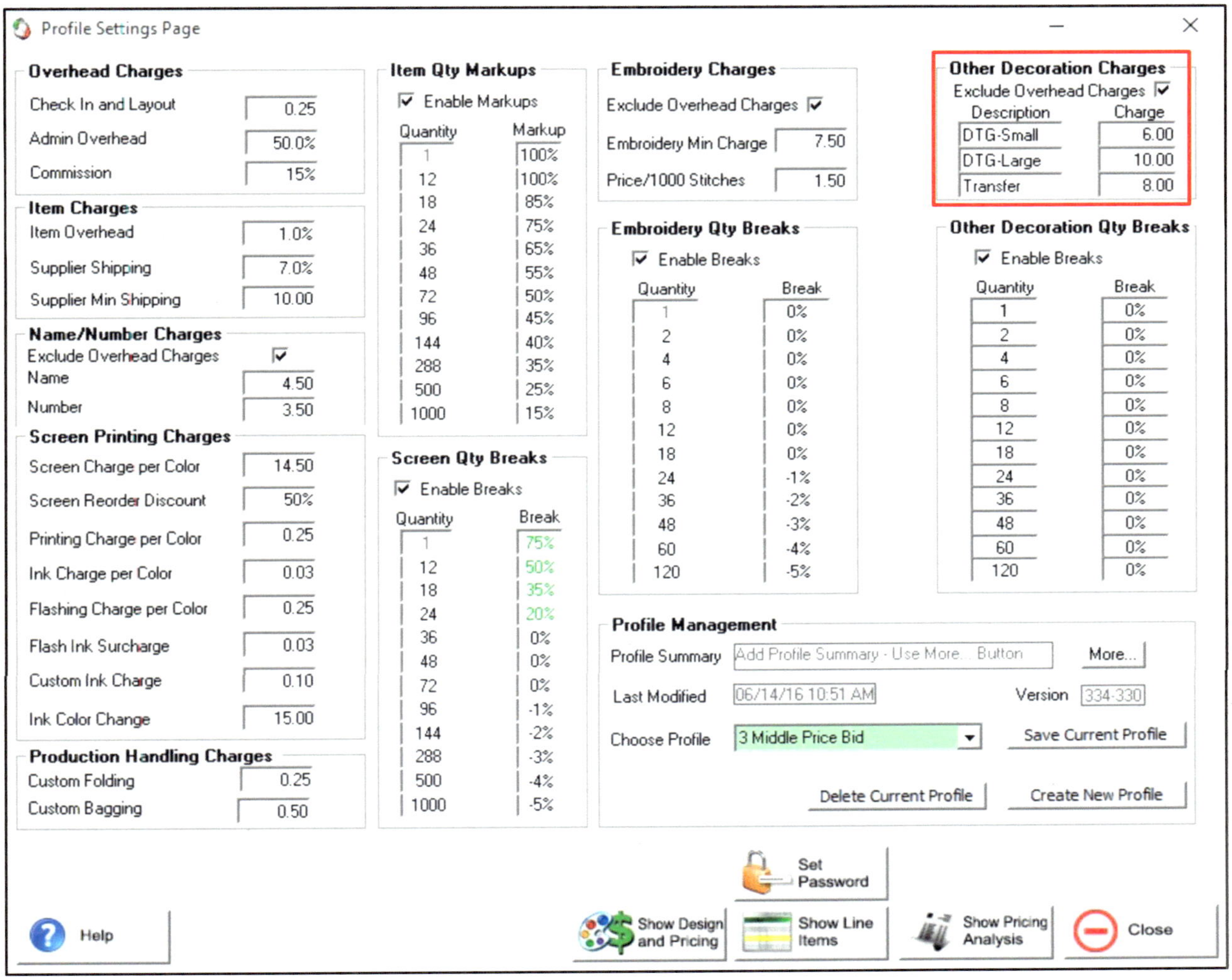

Whatever you put in the fields for the column **Description** becomes the field labels on the Design and Pricing Page. This allows you to specify decoration tasks on a profile-by-profile basis. For example, if you sell rhinestone decorations, consider having an Other Decoration

Charges area with choices for Rhinestones – Small, Rhinestones – Medium, and Rhinestones – Large.

The screen shots below show an example of the Other Decoration values on the Profile Settings Page and how this looks on the Design and Pricing Page and the Line Items Page.

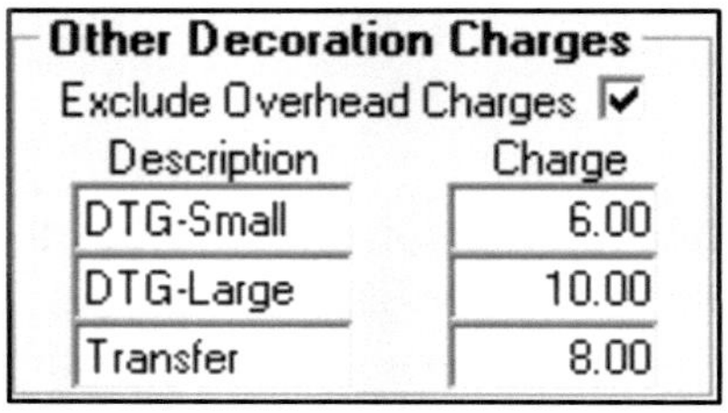

Profile Settings Page

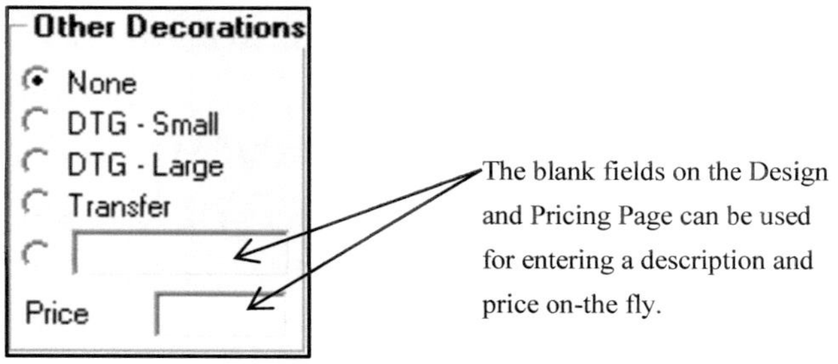

Design and Pricing Page

Other Decoration quantity breaks

The **Other Decoration Qty Breaks** table, which is at the right side of the Settings Page, lets you set up price breaks to provide a discount on the other decoration charges as the quantity increases.

The percentages in the **Other Decoration Qty Breaks** fields are calculated pricing adjustments and can be either a surcharge or a discount. Entering a positive number is treated as a surcharge. This feature can be useful for small quantities to ensure that you are adequately compensated for the time it takes to set up the job.

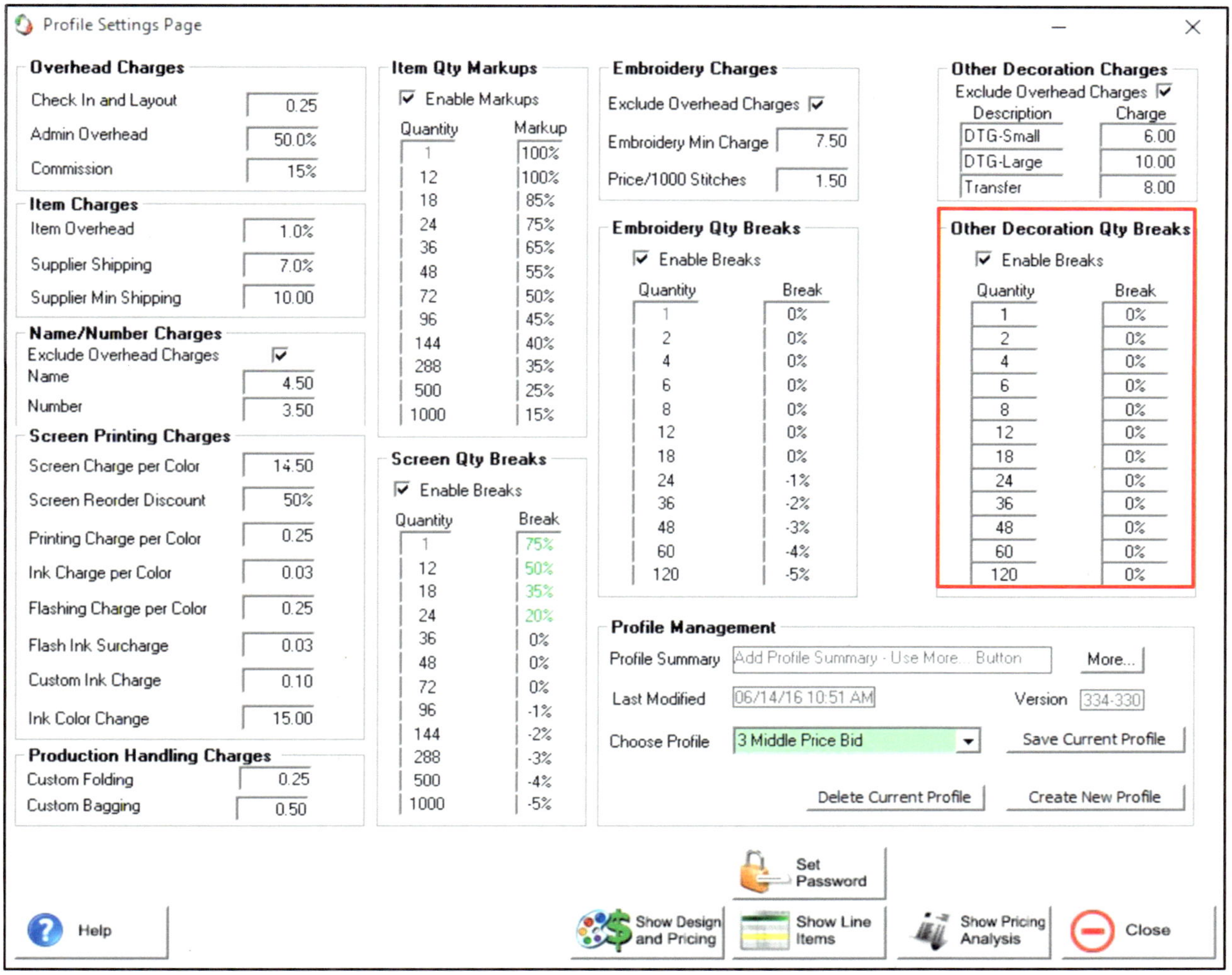

Things to Note

- Enter a positive amount to provide a surcharge. For example, if you have a 10 item minimum but occasionally make exceptions, consider entering a surcharge for quantities of less than 10 items.
- Positive percentages in the other decoration quantity breaks table are displayed in green to indicate that they will be treated as a surcharge.
- Enter a negative amount to provide a discount. For example, enter **-5** to give a 5% discount.
- If you turn off this feature (by unselecting the **Enable Breaks** check box at the top of this area), no price breaks are applied to the screen printing charges, regardless of the quantity for the line item.

Creating new pricing profiles

To create a new pricing profile,

1. Open the Fast Accurate Bids Profile Settings Page.
2. In the **Profile Management** area of the Profile Settings Page, click **Create New Profile**.

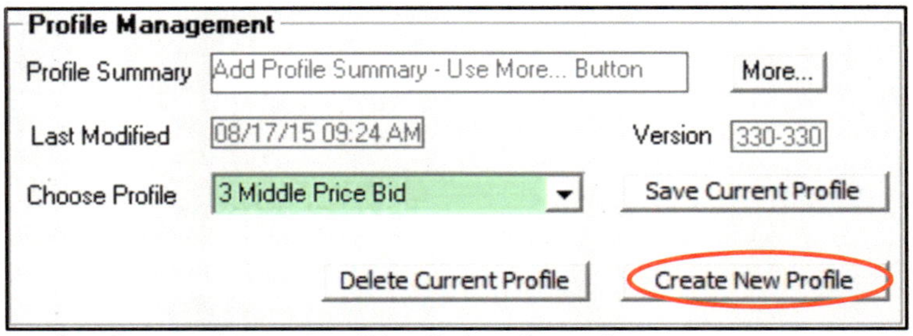

3. In the Create New Profile dialog box that appears, enter the name for the new pricing profile and click **Save**.
   At this point, you have created the new pricing profile that uses the currently displayed values.
4. Make any changes you want to the values on the Profile Settings Page.
5. Click **Save Profile** and click **OK** to the confirmation message that appears.

Things to Note:

- You are not limited in the number of pricing profiles that can be set up for Fast Accurate Bids.
- You can save a pricing profile to any alpha-numeric name and also use a blank space, and a dollar sign ($) in the name. You cannot use other special characters like the ampersand (&) or semicolon (;) in pricing profile names.
- The saved file will be written to **My Documents/Fast Accurate Bids/Pricing Profiles** and have the file extension **.pro**. For example, if you create a pricing profile called "Schools and Non Profits," the file will be named **Schools and Non Profits.pro**.
- The **My Documents/Fast Accurate Bids/Pricing Profiles** folder also stores a copy of the build-in pricing profiles. You can use the built-in pricing profiles to create bids, and to create your custom pricing profiles, but you cannot make changes to their settings. The built-in pricing profiles get overwritten by the latest version of the built-in profiles when you update your software.
- The profiles you create and store in the pricing profiles folder are protected from being removed when you install updates to the Fast Accurate Bids software.

Sharing pricing profiles

When you create a pricing profile through Fast Accurate Bids, it's saved on your computer in the directory location **My Documents/Fast Accurate Bids/Pricing Profiles** with the pricing profile name you assigned it and the file extension **.pro**. The pricing profile (**.pro**) files are binary files and can only be used from within the Fast Accurate Bids software.

An important feature to keep in mind, however, is that you can share the pricing profile files with other Fast Accurate Bids users.

One of the easiest ways to share your pricing profiles is to send them as an attachment to an email and have the person you send them to save the attached files to the **My Documents/Fast Accurate Bids/Pricing Profiles** folder on their computer. You can also copy them to a thumb drive or use any of the other ways that Windows allows users to copy files from one computer to another.

Once a **.pro** file has been copied to profiles folder, the next time that Fast Accurate Bids is started the newly added pricing profile will be available for use just as if it had been originally created using that version of Fast Accurate Bids.

Suggestions for sharing pricing profiles

- **Save time and ensure pricing consistency**
  If you have multiple copies of Fast Accurate Bids for use in your business, you can save time and ensure pricing consistency by developing the set of pricing profiles that you want used and then sending those profiles to your other users.

- **Streamline pricing for your sales partners**
  If you are a contract decorator for companies that take apparel decoration orders, you can send them your pricing profiles so that they are self-sufficient in knowing what their pricing will be.

- **Protect your pricing privacy**
  If you are concerned about the privacy of your pricing data with regard to your employees or contractors, activate the Fast Accurate Bids password protection feature on their versions of the software so that they cannot open the Profile Settings Page to view the pricing profiles you send them.

- **Compare pricing from multiple contract printers**
  If your company takes apparel decoration orders and uses multiple contract decorators, have them send you their pricing profiles so that you can compare their prices and select the best pricing for specific orders.

- **Safeguard your pricing**
  Consider saving a backup of your set of pricing profiles to a safe place that is off site from your business so that if there is ever a fire or other disaster at your shop, you will not lose the pricing information that you've developed for your business.

Deleting pricing profiles

To delete a pricing profile,

1. Open the Fast Accurate Bids Profile Settings Page, and in the Profile Management Settings area of the Profile Settings Page, click the down-arrow to the right of the pricing profile name.

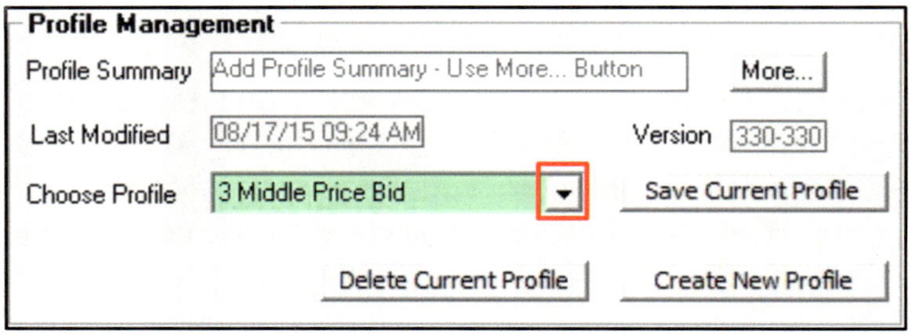

2. From the list of pricing profiles, select the one that you want to delete.

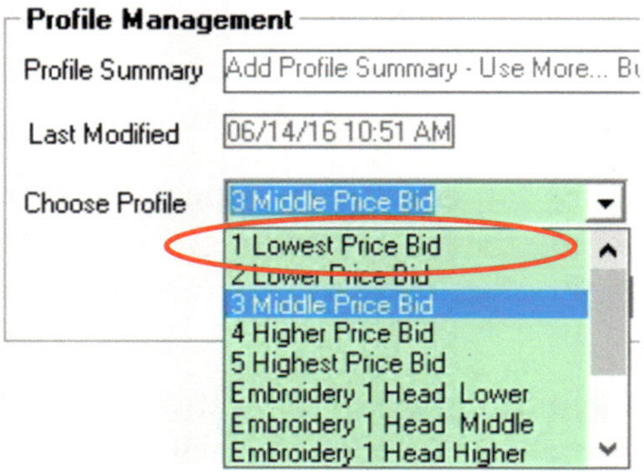

3. Click **Delete Current Profile**.

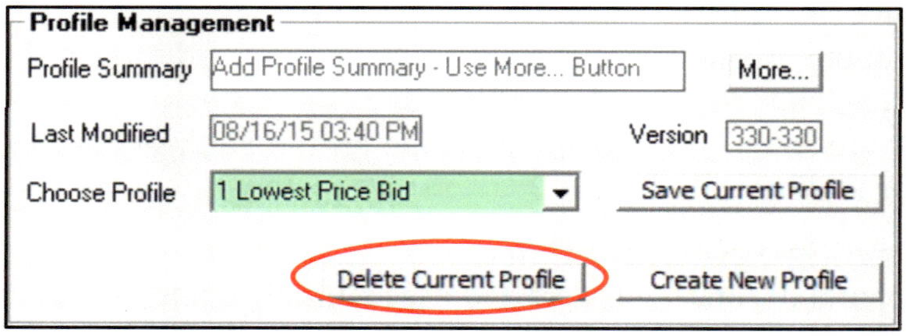

4. Click **Yes** to the prompt for permission to delete the pricing profile.
5. Click **OK** to the message that the pricing profile has been deleted.

Things to note:

- Consider deleting the built-in pricing profiles that you don't want to keep around for use in creating bids.

- Fast Accurate Bids requires the existence of at least one pricing profile to run properly. If you have only one pricing profile left, Fast Accurate Bids does not let you delete it from within the program.
- If all the profiles get deleted from **My Documents/Fast Accurate Bids/Profiles**, Fast Accurate Bids will alert you regarding the condition the next time it starts and restore the set of built-in profiles to the **Profiles** folder.
- If you're hesitant to delete a pricing profile because you are concerned about possibly needing it at a later time, consider creating a folder under **My Documents/Fast Accurate Bids/Profiles** called something like "Obsolete Profiles" and moving the pricing profiles you don't want on your profiles list to that location. Fast Accurate Bids only displays the pricing profiles that it finds in the folder **My Documents/Fast Accurate Bids/Profiles**.

Supplier connectors

"Supplier connector" is the generic name for the programs included in Fast Accurate Bids that let you update the electronic pricing files available from your wholesale suppliers. This set of programs is built into the software and can only be used from the Fast Accurate Bids Choose Item Page.

Performing the initial update of your supplier prices and keeping your pricing files current is an important step in ensuring that your bids are accurate. Fast Accurate Bids provides step-by-step instructions in the section called Updating supplier pricing files in this manual, and supplier-specific instructions in the online help within the Fast Accurate Bids software.

There is a display field in the Find Supplier Item area of the Choose Item Page that displays how long it's been since you last updated the currently selected supplier's pricing file.

This field displays how long it's been since the currently selected supplier's pricing file was last updated.

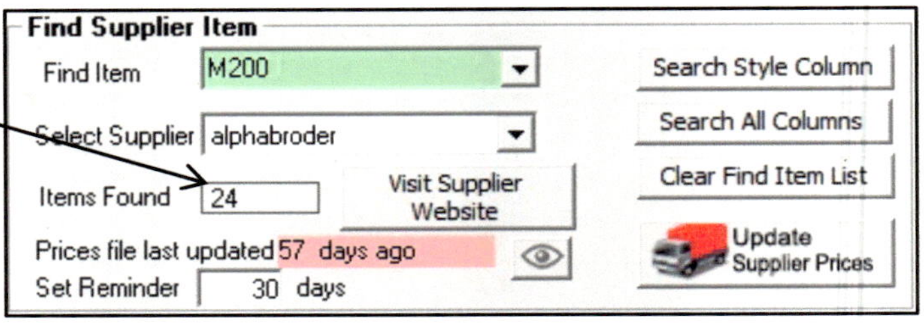

If there is pink highlighting on the number of days since the supplier pricing file was last updated, it means that the number of days since the pricing file was last updated has exceeded the setting for the Connector Update Reminder in the field **Set Reminder**.

It is up to you to make sure that your pricing data is current. The **Set Reminder** field lets you specify how frequently the reminder appears but it is up to you to update the pricing information for the wholesale suppliers you use.

Switching between suppliers

At the bottom of the Choose Item Page there is a drop-down list for switching between suppliers. This list displays the supplier connectors available for use with Fast Accurate Bids.

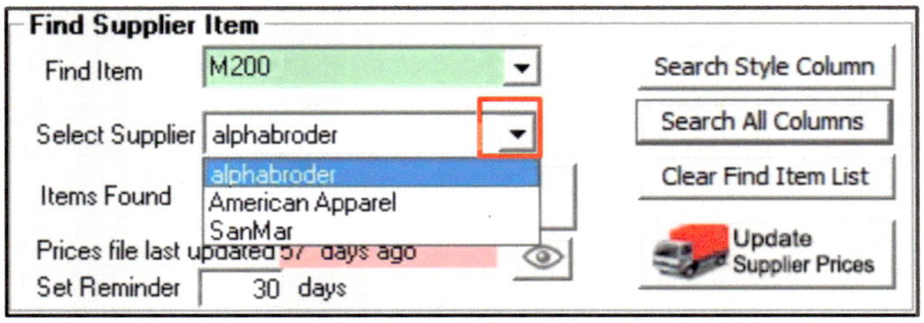

Note: Fast Accurate Bids offers supplier connectors for SanMar, American Apparel and alphabroder. We realize that there are many excellent suppliers serving apparel decoration businesses in addition to these companies. We will be adding more supplier connectors and welcome your suggestions on the ones that would be the most valuable to you.

Updating supplier pricing files

The steps that follow describe the process for using a supplier connector to update a pricing file in Fast Accurate Bids. It is based on using the Windows System 7 operating system and Chrome Explorer. If you use a different Windows operating system, the update steps may be somewhat different.

Note: Steps 4 through 10 use SanMar as an example of how to perform this process. The section in this manual called Supplier download instructions provides a table with summary information on where to find the download file on the suppliers' websites and the settings to choose. For more detailed documentation on the download process for each specific supplier, click the **Help** button on the Update Supplier Pricing dialog box.

To update a pricing file,

1. On the Choose Item Page, click **Update Supplier Prices**.

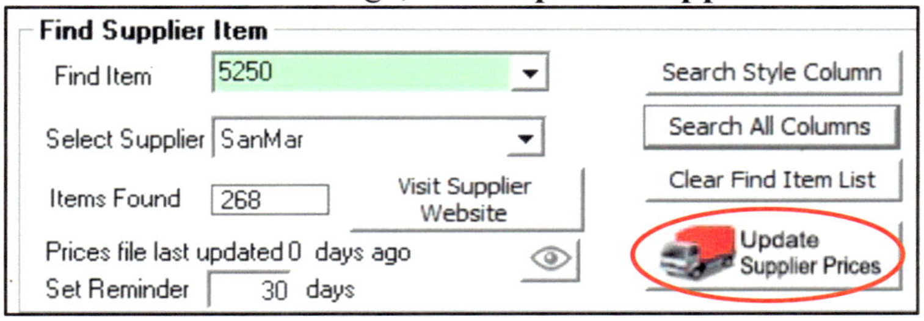

2. In the Update Supplier Prices dialog box that appears, select the supplier that you want to update from the Supplier Options dropdown list.

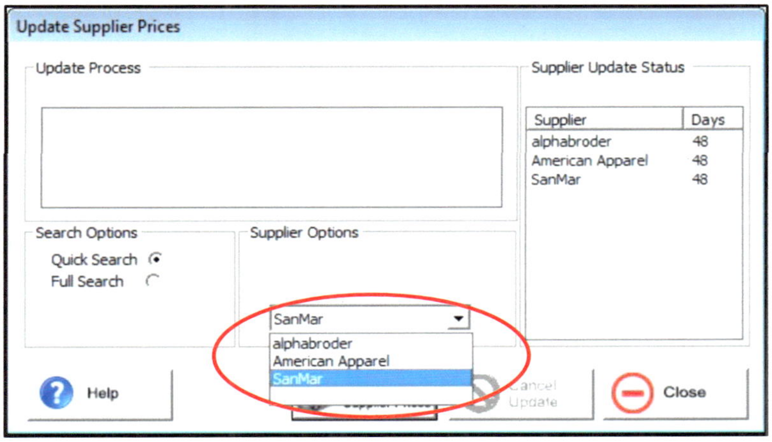

3. You can save a lot of time in the update process by leaving the Search Options choice set to **Quick Search**.

   Note: **Quick Search** searches just your Windows downloads folder for the downloaded pricing file and **Full Search** searches your entire hard drive. If you intend to save your supplier's pricing file to a folder other than the Windows Downloads folder, choose **Full Search**.

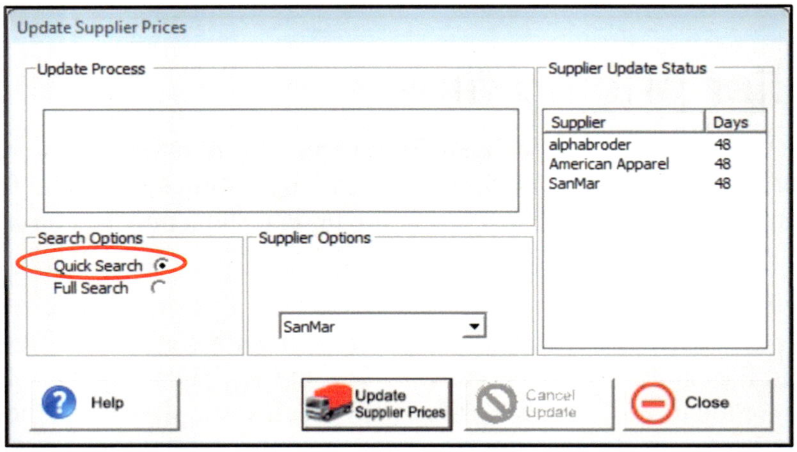

4. Click **Update Supplier Prices**.

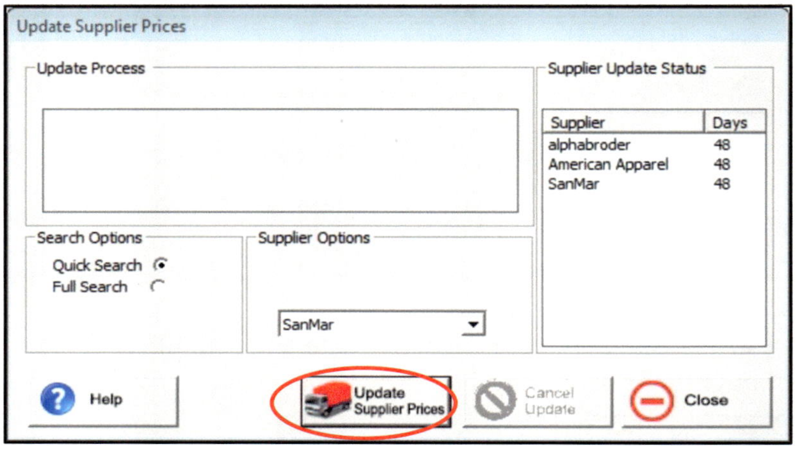

5. Click **Continue** to the confirmation dialog box that appears. This will take you to your supplier's login page.

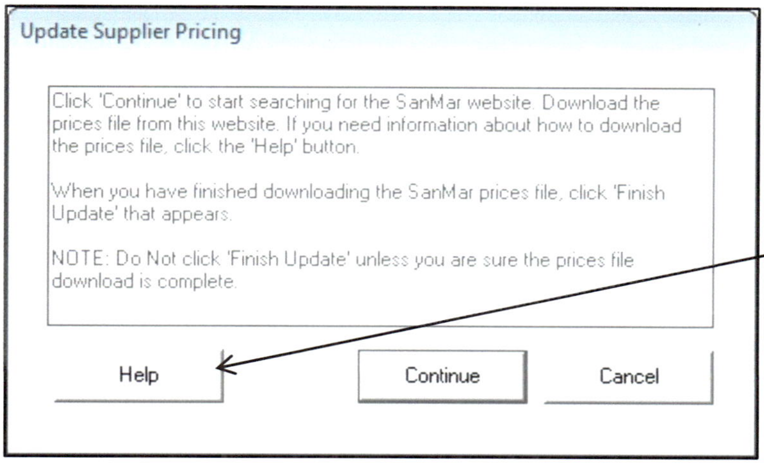

If you need help on where to find the pricing files on the supplier's website or what options to choose for the download, click **Help**.

Note: Some suppliers, for example SanMar, allow you to stay logged in. If this is the case, disregard step 6.

6. Log into the supplier's website using your regular customer login information.

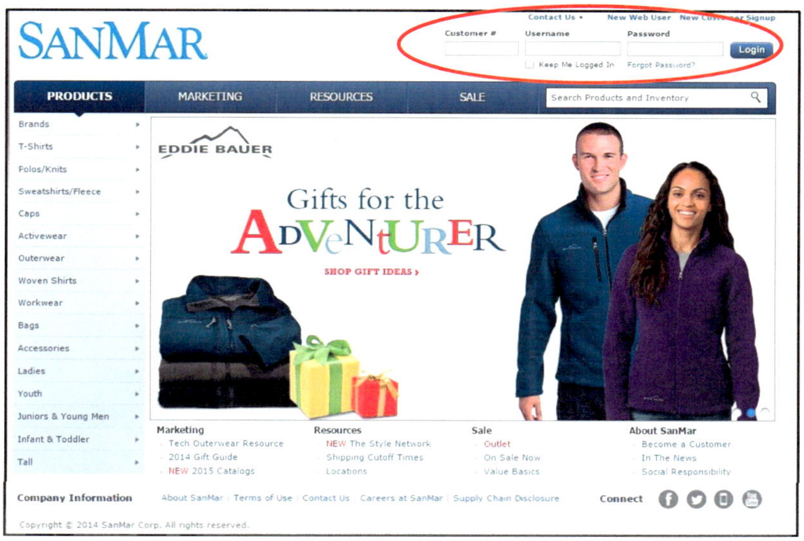

Note: If you're not yet a customer of the supplier, you must set up an account with them to update their pricing.

7. Navigate to the pricing file download page on the website.
   For example, for SanMar the path to this file is **Resources | SanMar Data Library.**

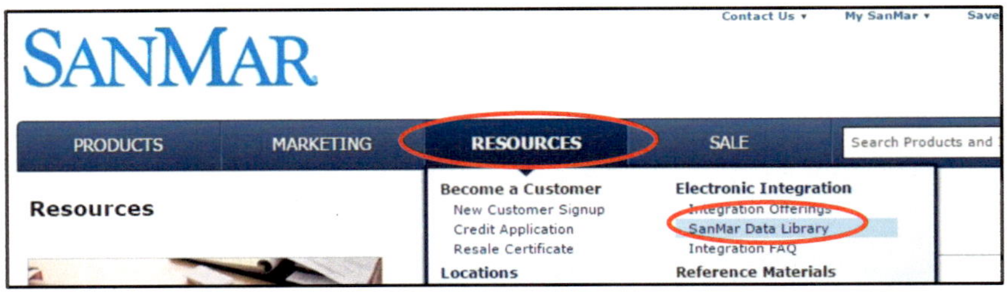

See the section in this manual called Supplier download instructions for information on where to find the download link on suppliers' websites.

8. On the supplier's website, select the choices for downloading the prices file. For example, for SanMar, on the Product Information Download Page, make the choices shown below for this step.

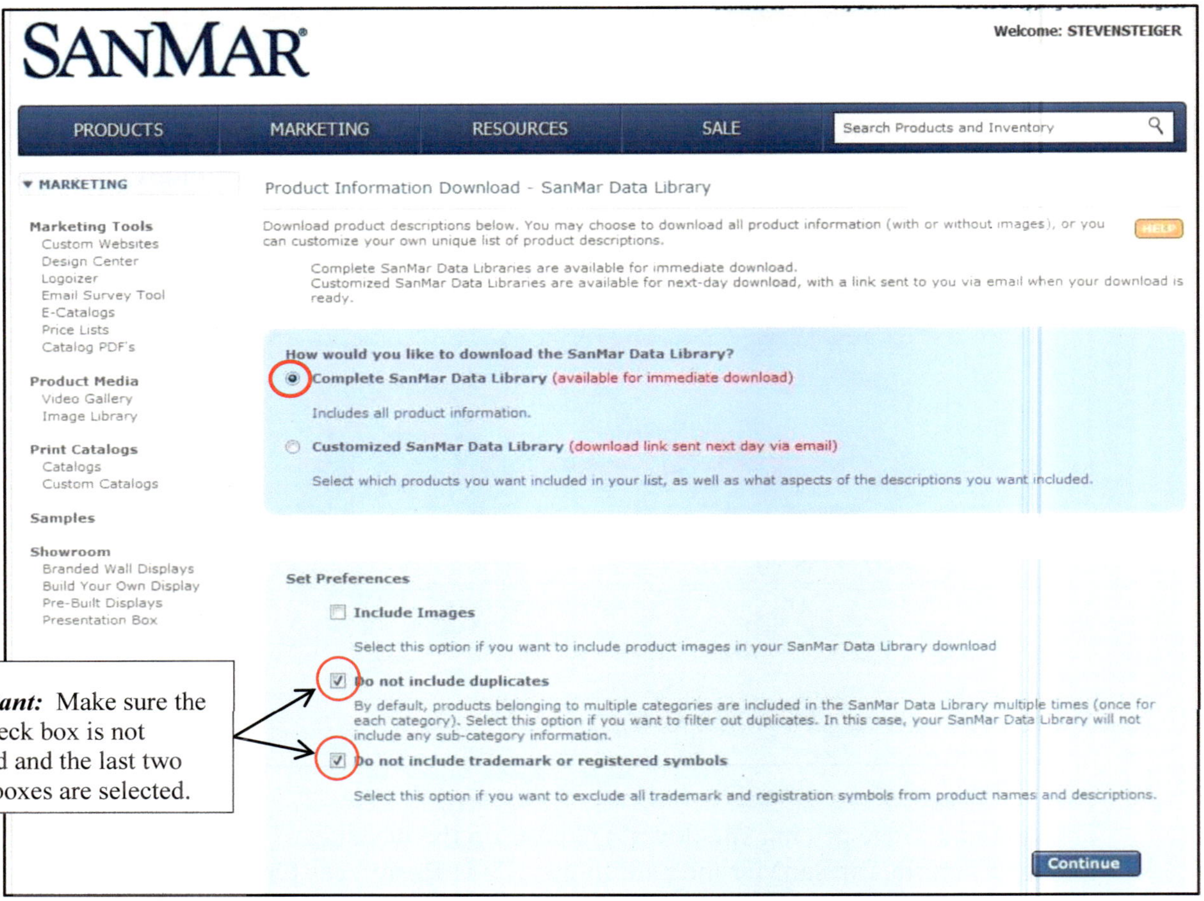

Important: Make sure the first check box is not selected and the last two check boxes are selected.

9. Click **Continue**.
10. On the next screen that appears, choose **I Accept** and click **Begin Download**.

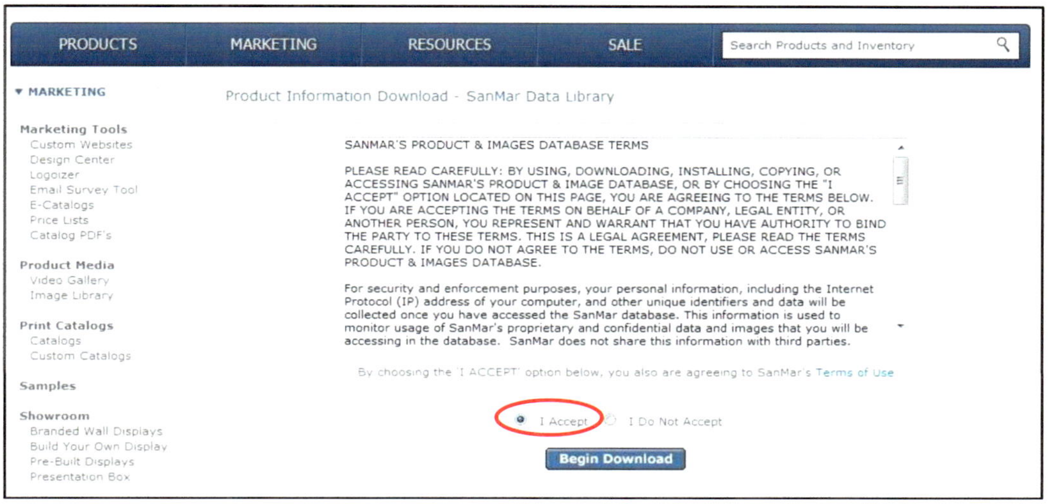

11. In the dialog box that appears, select **Save**.

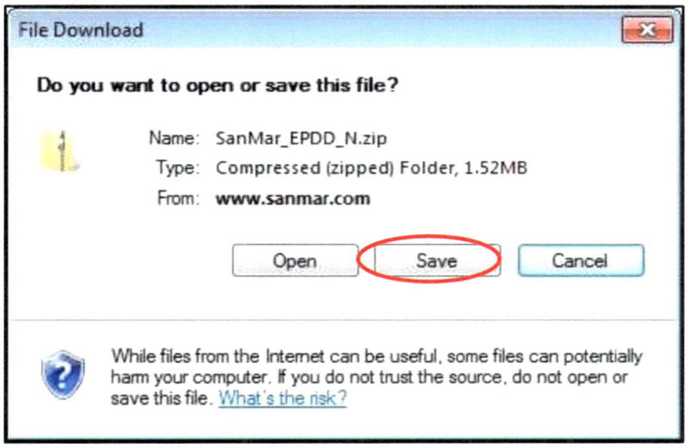

Note: The steps in this procedure are based on the Windows 7 and Internet Explorer. If you use a different Windows OS, a different web browser, or different settings for your downloads procedure the information in the Windows dialog boxes may vary slightly.

Note: In the Downloads dialog box that appears, a progress bar tracks the file download process and shows an icon for the file when the download is complete. Keep in mind, however, that if you have a fast connection the process may complete so quickly that you may never see the progress bar.

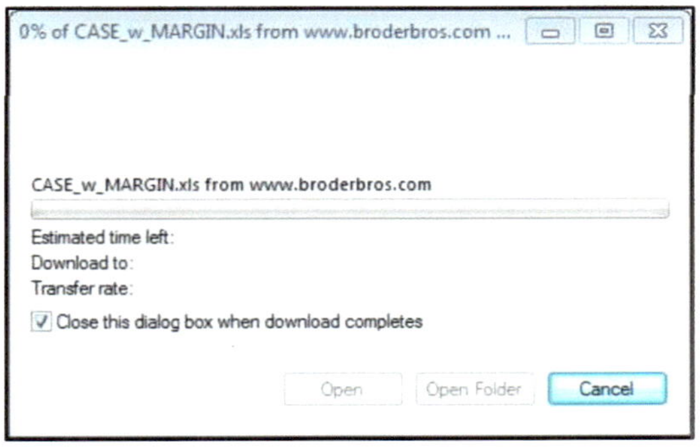

12. When Windows displays the Save As dialog box, click **Save**.

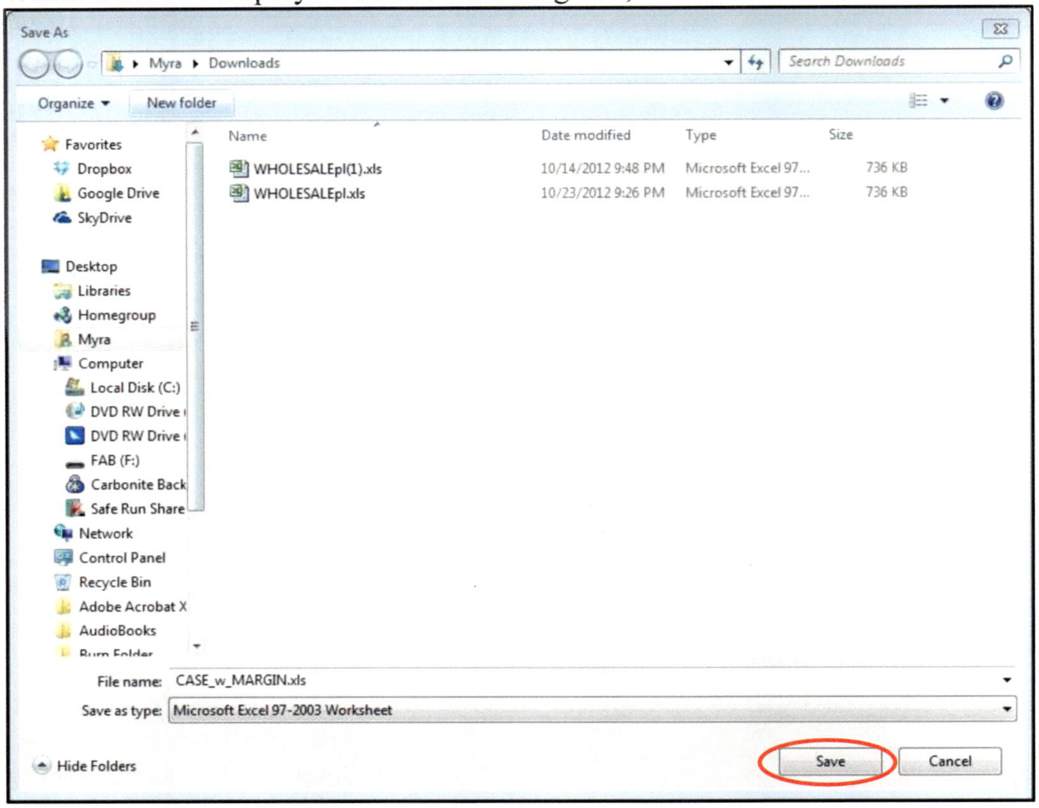

Internet Explorer displays an additional message box that shows the progress as it saves the file to your computer.

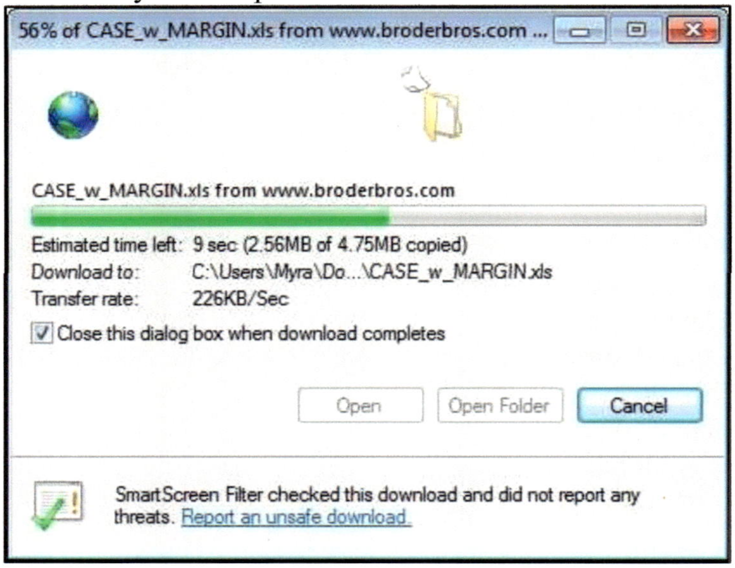

Important: Do not open the pricing file. Just save it.

Once the file has been saved, this message box closes automatically.

13. Close the SanMar web page. Then, click **Finish Update** in the Fast Accurate Bids Update Supplier Pricing dialog box.

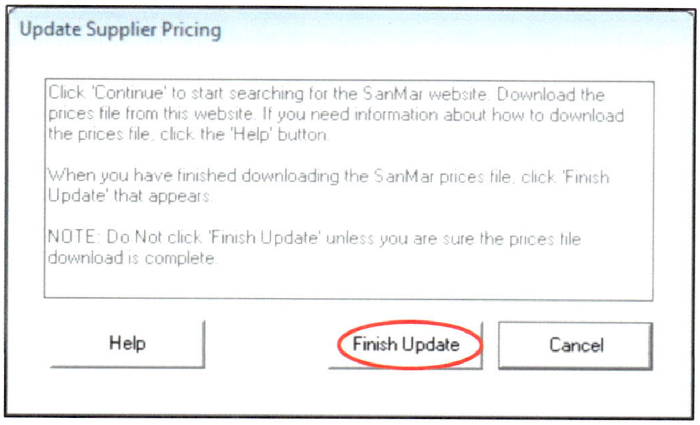

From this point forward the Fast Accurate Bids software automatically takes control of the process of updating the pricing file. You will see a series of messages as each step completes.

Note: If you selected **Full Search** in step 3, please be patient while the update process searches the folders on your computer for the pricing file you just downloaded. This step can take as much as several minutes to complete. You will see the **Searching Folders** field count the folders as it looks for the file that you just downloaded. The counting proceeds from folder to folder, so what may appear to be a long pause in the counting simply means that the search process encountered a windows folder with a large number of files in it.

14. Fast Accurate Bids displays a completion message when the process is done. Click **OK** to close the message box.

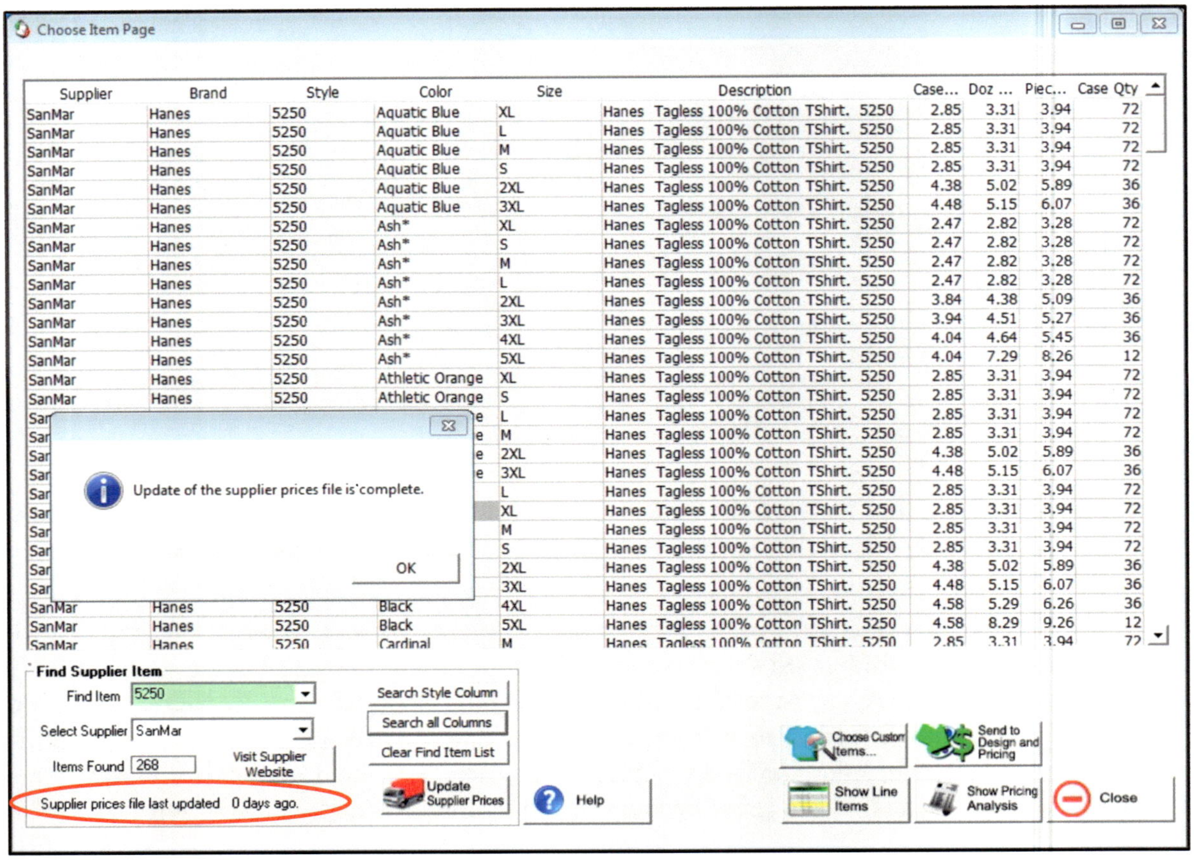

At this point, you have updated the supplier's pricing file and the updated data is available for use.

Note that in the Supplier Update Status on the Choose Item Page now shows that the supplier prices file was last updated 0 days ago.

Note: Fast Accurate Bids automatically removes the downloaded pricing file as cleanup step for the pricing update process so that you do not start accumulating lots of large data files in your downloads directory.

Supplier download instructions

The table that follows provides brief instructions on where to look on the supplier websites to access the link for downloading their pricing file and the selection choices to make to get the correct data for the Fast Accurate Bids supplier connector.

You must have an account with the suppliers before you will be able to download their pricing file.

Supplier	Website location	Download choices to take
American Apparel	Contact American Apparel for their prices website.	Excel
alphabroder	www.alphabroder.com Marketing Engine Catalogs Download Price Lists	On the Price Lists Page, click **Download the most current alphabroder price lists**. On the Downloadable Excels and PDFs Page, click **Main Catalog** **Wholesale** **Excel**
SanMar	www.sanmar.com Resources SanMar Data Library	Complete SanMar Data Library Do not include duplicates Do not include trademark or registered symbols

Setting up a reminder to update pricing

When the number of days that you specify has elapsed, the number of days in the field **Prices file last updated** on the Choose Item Page is highlighted in red.

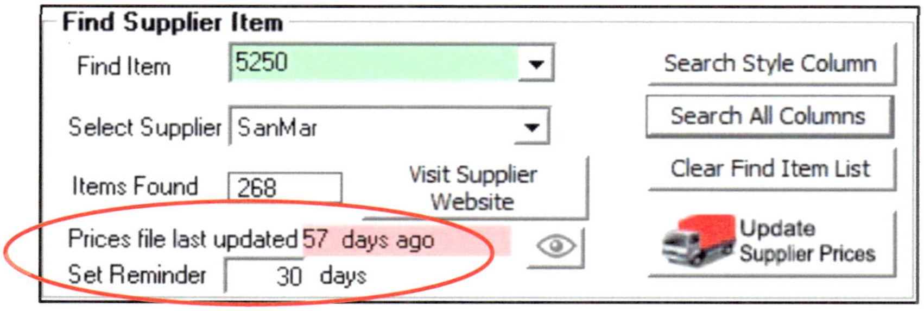

To set up a reminder for updating your pricing profiles, enter a count-down number in the field **Set Reminder** for how frequently you want to be reminded to update your pricing profiles.

The reminder is specific to each supplier. This lets you can set up a different number of days for the reminder for each of your suppliers.

Custom items

Within Fast Accurate Bids, the term "custom items" means any items that you cannot select from the Choose Item Page because you do not have access to a supplier connector for the company from which you intend to order them.

The Custom Items Page lets you set up and manage your list of custom items for use on bids.

When you add a custom item to the Design and Pricing Page, Fast Accurate Bids treats the custom item in the same manner as an item selected from the Choose Item Page.

Adding custom items

To add items to the Custom Items Page,

1. On the Design and Pricing Page, click the **Choose Custom Item** button.
2. On the Custom Item Page, click the **Add New Row** button to add an additional blank row to the top of the table.
3. Enter the item information for the custom item in the blank row at the top of the table.
4. Repeat steps 2 and 3 until you've added all the custom items that you want.
5. When you're done, click **Save Custom List** and close the page.

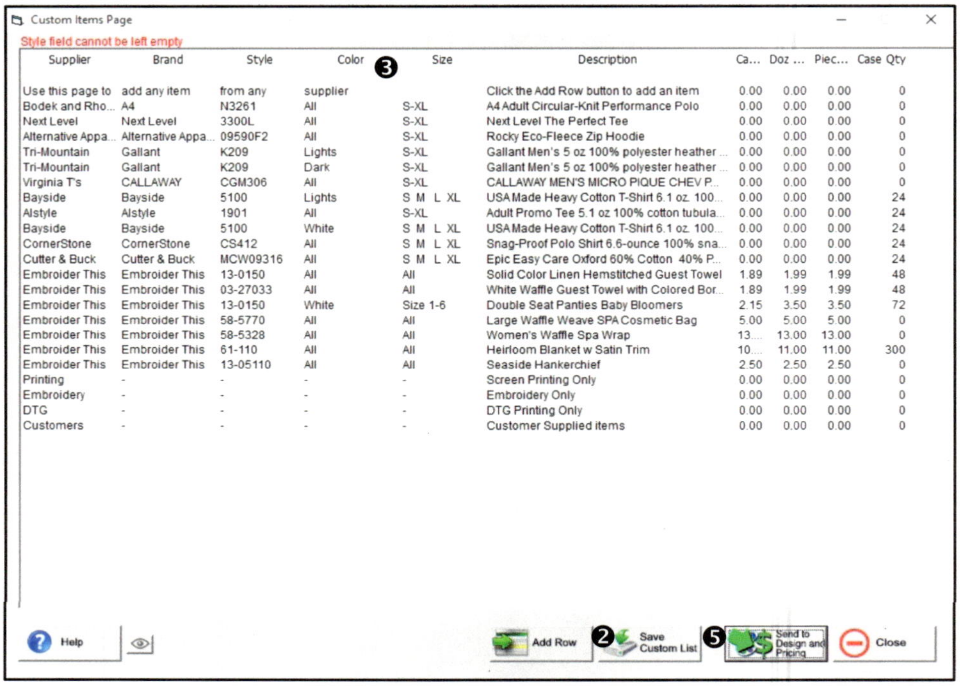

Supplier	Brand	Style	Color	Size	Description	Ca...	Doz ...	Piec...	Case Qty
Use this page to	add any item	from any	supplier		Click the Add Row button to add an item	0.00	0.00	0.00	0
Bodek and Rho...	A4	N3261	All	S-XL	A4 Adult Circular-Knit Performance Polo	0.00	0.00	0.00	0
Next Level	Next Level	3300L	All	S-XL	Next Level The Perfect Tee	0.00	0.00	0.00	0
Alternative Appa...	Alternative Appa...	09590F2	All	S-XL	Rocky Eco-Fleece Zip Hoodie	0.00	0.00	0.00	0
Tri-Mountain	Gallant	K209	Lights	S-XL	Gallant Men's 5 oz 100% polyester heather ...	0.00	0.00	0.00	0
Tri-Mountain	Gallant	K209	Dark	S-XL	Gallant Men's 5 oz 100% polyester heather ...	0.00	0.00	0.00	0
Virginia T's	CALLAWAY	CGM306	All	S-XL	CALLAWAY MEN'S MICRO PIQUE CHEV P...	0.00	0.00	0.00	0
Bayside	Bayside	5100	Lights	S M L XL	USA Made Heavy Cotton T-Shirt 6.1 oz. 100...	0.00	0.00	0.00	24
Alstyle	Alstyle	1901	All	S-XL	Adult Promo Tee 5.1 oz 100% cotton tubula...	0.00	0.00	0.00	24
Bayside	Bayside	5100	White	S M L XL	USA Made Heavy Cotton T-Shirt 6.1 oz. 100...	0.00	0.00	0.00	24
CornerStone	CornerStone	CS412	All	S M L XL	Snag-Proof Polo Shirt 6.6-ounce 100% sna...	0.00	0.00	0.00	24
Cutter & Buck	Cutter & Buck	MCW09316	All	S M L XL	Epic Easy Care Oxford 60% Cotton 40% P...	0.00	0.00	0.00	24
Embroider This	Embroider This	13-0150	All	All	Solid Color Linen Hemstitched Guest Towel	1.89	1.99	1.99	48
Embroider This	Embroider This	03-27033	All	All	White Waffle Guest Towel with Colored Bor...	1.89	1.99	1.99	48
Embroider This	Embroider This	13-0150	White	Size 1-6	Double Seat Panties Baby Bloomers	2.15	3.50	3.50	72
Embroider This	Embroider This	58-5770	All	All	Large Waffle Weave SPA Cosmetic Bag	5.00	5.00	5.00	0
Embroider This	Embroider This	58-5328	All	All	Women's Waffle Spa Wrap	13....	13.00	13.00	0
Embroider This	Embroider This	61-110	All	All	Heirloom Blanket w Satin Trim	10....	11.00	11.00	300
Embroider This	Embroider This	13-05110	All	All	Seaside Hankerchief	2.50	2.50	2.50	0
Printing	-	-	-	-	Screen Printing Only	0.00	0.00	0.00	0
Embroidery	-	-	-	-	Embroidery Only	0.00	0.00	0.00	0
DTG	-	-	-	-	DTG Printing Only	0.00	0.00	0.00	0
Customers	-	-	-	-	Customer Supplied items	0.00	0.00	0.00	0

Things to note

- The only required field is **Style**, but if you do not add information in the other fields, the corresponding fields will be blank when you send the information to the Line Items Page.
- To sort the information on the custom items list, click in the column heading of the column to sort by.
- A custom item with the description **Items supplied by customer** is provided for use when printing items supplied by your customer.

- When creating bids, you can add a custom item on-the-fly by opening the Custom Item Page, entering the new custom item and then right-clicking and choosing **Send to Design and Pricing Page** from the menu that appears. Fast Accurate Bids will automatically save the list and close the Custom Items Page for you.

Removing custom items

To remove one or more custom items from the Custom Items Page,

1. Open the Custom Items Page and right-click in the row for the item you want to remove from the table.
2. Select **Delete row** from the context menu that appears.
3. Click **Yes** to the prompt to delete the row.

Sharing the custom items

If you have multiple copies of Fast Accurate Bids for use in your business, you can save time and ensure consistency by maintaining your custom items information using a designated specific computer in your business and then sending the updates for the custom items information to your other users.

The custom items file, **Custom Items.csv,** is located in the directory **Documents/Fast Accurate Bids/Data**. The easiest way to share this file is to send it as an attachment to an email and have the people you sent it to save the attached files to the **My Documents/Fast Accurate Bids/Data Files** folder on their computer. You can also copy the custom items file to a thumb drive or use any of the other ways that Windows allows users to copy files from one computer to another.

Once **Custom Itmes.csv** has been copied to **My Documents/Fast Accurate Bids/Data Files**, the next time that Fast Accurate Bids is started the newly added custom items will be available for use just as if they had been added using that version of Fast Accurate Bids.

Important: Although the custom items file is a .csv file, we strongly advise again editing this file directly. Fast Accurate Bids will not provide support for problems that arise from editing this file directly.

Microsoft Word Template

The Fast Accurate Bids software has an associated Microsoft Word template that generates the Word file to which the line items table and customer contact information is copied. This is the last step in creating the bid.

The template is called **Fast Accurate Bids Template.dotx** and is located in the folder **My Documents/Fast Accurate Bids/Documents**.

Adapting the template to your company

1. Open Microsoft Word and from the **File** menu open the file **My Documents/Fast Accurate Bids/Documents/Fast Accurate Bids Template.dotx**.
   Note: You must open the file by selecting **Open** from the **File** menu. Attempting to open a Word template by double-clicking on it will result in opening it as a document file.
2. Add the letterhead for your company to the top of the page.
3. Edit or replace the text with standard information that you provide when you send a bid to a customer.
   Important: Do not delete the words **For:** and **Date:** at the top of the file or **<Estimate>**, which is toward the end of the file. These are special terms that the Fast Accurate Bids software uses to incorporate the bid information into the file.
4. When you have finished the edits you want to make to this file, select **Save As** from the File menu, save the changes and close the file.

Things to Note

- In case you need it, Fast Accurate Bids provides a backup copy of the word template in **My Documents/Fast Accurate Bids** called **Fast Accurate Bids Template (copy).dotx.**
- The template supplied by the program can only be used with Word 2007 and later. If you have an earlier version of Word that uses **.dot** templates, you can click the **Send Bid to Clipboard** button on the Line Items Page to copy the line items table and paste it into a document that you have created.
- Consider adding information to the Word template that lists the charges that are inclusive in your bid. For example, "Our prices include everything – shirts, artwork, digitizing, and embroidery. Tax is extra."

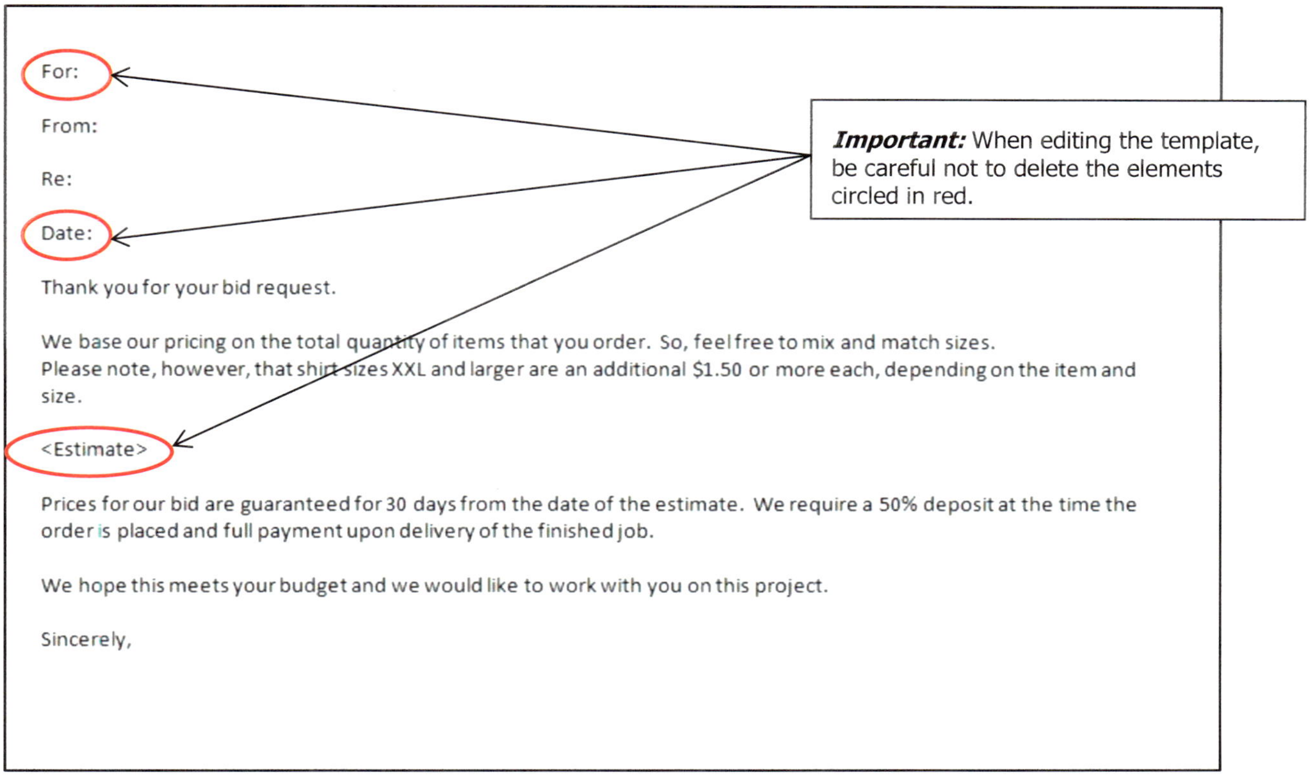
For:

From:

Re:

Date:

Thank you for your bid request.

We base our pricing on the total quantity of items that you order. So, feel free to mix and match sizes.
Please note, however, that shirt sizes XXL and larger are an additional $1.50 or more each, depending on the item and size.

<Estimate>

Prices for our bid are guaranteed for 30 days from the date of the estimate. We require a 50% deposit at the time the order is placed and full payment upon delivery of the finished job.

We hope this meets your budget and we would like to work with you on this project.

Sincerely,

Sharing the template with other users

If you have multiple copies of Fast Accurate Bids for use in your business, you can save time and ensure consistency by editing the Microsoft Word template once and then sharing the edited version of the template with the other users.

One of the easiest ways to share the template is to send it as an attachment to an email and have the people you send it to save it to the **My Documents/Fast Accurate Bids/Documents** folder on their computer. You can also copy it to a thumb drive or use any of the other ways that Windows allows users to copy files from one computer to another.

Important: Once the template has been copied to another computer, it's important to have the recipient right-click and open the template and then save it. This establishes the ownership of the Word file on the recipient's computer so that it can be used successfully from Fast Accurate Bids.

Using password protection

If you don't want to allow your staff to make changes to your pricing profiles or view your pricing information, you can set up password protection to block their access to the Profile Settings Page, the Pricing Analysis Page, and the Program Preferences dialog box.

How password protection works

When you set a password in Fast Accurate Bids, you are actually setting the ability for the software to run in either Owner mode or User mode.

Owner mode means that the Design and Pricing Page continues to provide buttons to access the Profile Settings Page and the Pricing Analysis page as if the program does not use a password.

User mode means that these buttons have been removed so that these pages cannot be opened and (unless the user is aware of using the program in Owner mode); he or she will not even know that they exist.

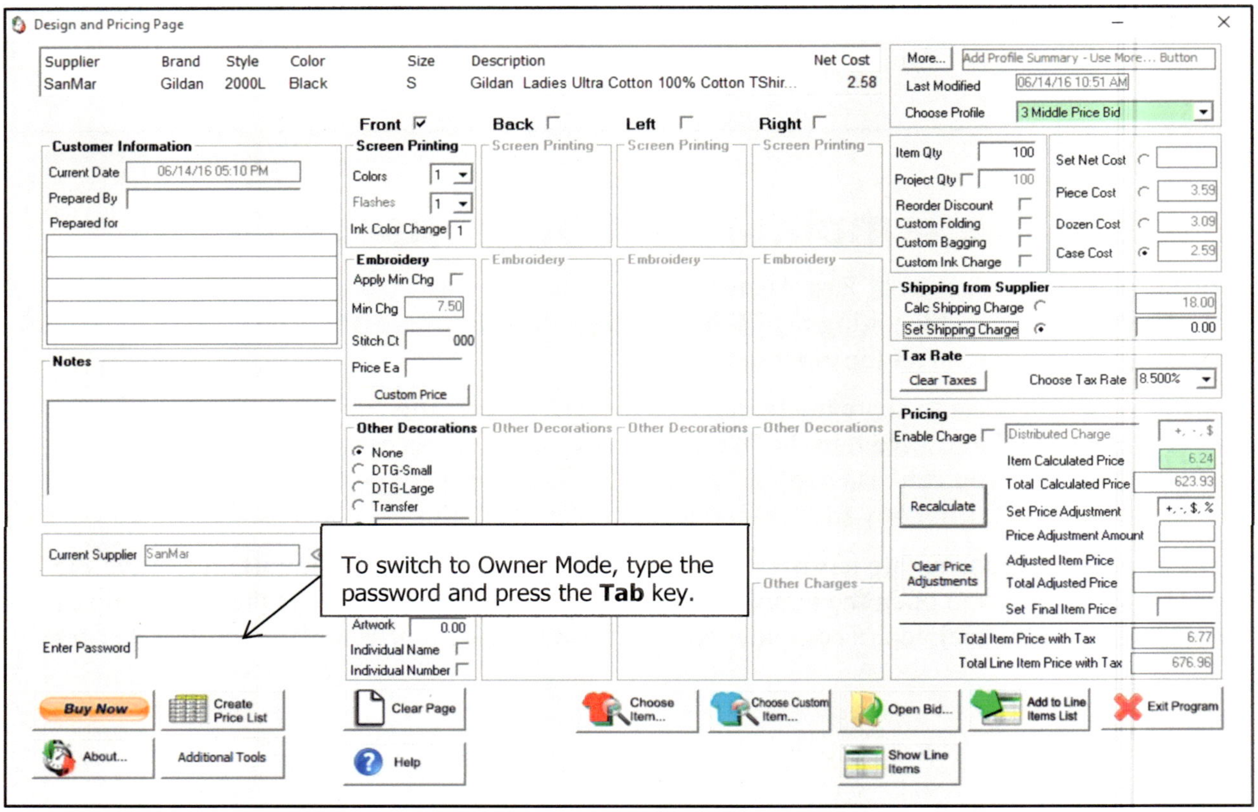

When you set a password for Fast Accurate Bids, you will see an additional field on the Design and Pricing Page that allows you to open the program in Owner mode. This field does not appear unless you have enabled password protection.

Before you set a password, the program will always open in Owner mode, which means the buttons accessing the Profile Settings Page and the Pricing Analysis Page will appear.

Once you set a password, the field **Enter Password** is added to the Design and Pricing Page. From that point forward, Fast Accurate Bids always starts in User mode but can be switched to Owner mode by entering the correct password. Keep in mind that passwords in Fast Accurate Bids are case sensitive.

Adding, changing, and removing a password

To add password protection,

1. Open the Fast Accurate Bids Profile Settings Page and click the Set Password button.

2. In the Set Password dialog box that appears, select the check box **Enable passwords** and enter the same password in the fields **Type Password** and **Confirm Password**.

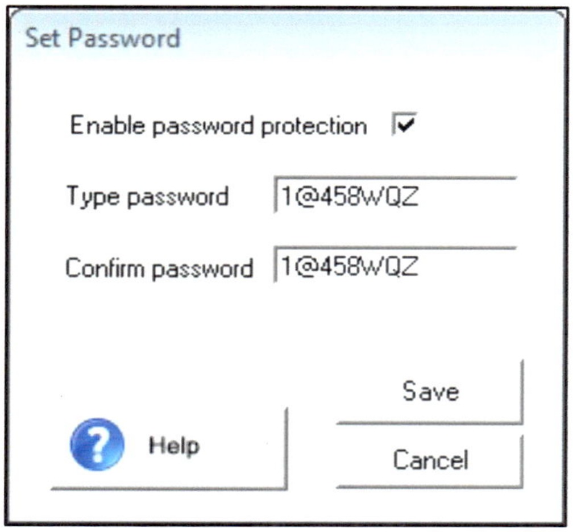

The default password is **password**. If you choose to use password protection, be sure to change this to a more secure password for you software.

Note: You can enter any alphanumeric string. You can also use spaces and the following special characters + - . $ & % # @ - _. The password is case sensitive, so when you set it up, keep in mind that it must be typed in exactly the same combination of capital and lower case letters as you originally entered it.

3. Click **Save Password** and close the Set Password dialog box.

Note: Password protection takes effect as soon as you click **Save**.

To change the password,

1. If password protection is enabled, then on the Design and Pricing Page, enter the password and press the Enter key.
2. Click **Settings** to open the Fast Accurate Bids Profile Settings Page, and click **Set Password**.
3. In the Set Password dialog box, select the current password and type the new password in the fields **Type password** and **Confirm password**.
4. Click **Save** and click OK to the confirmation message that appears.

To remove password protection from the program,

1. Enter the password on the Design and Pricing Page, and then click the **Settings** button that appears.
2. On Profile Settings Page that appears, click the Set Password button.
3. In the Set Password dialog box, unselect the **Enable password protection** check box.

Showing or hiding the item cost

If you do not want your item cost for items to be visible, you can turn off this display (and turn it back on again) using the show/hide item cost button (👁). This button appears on the Design and Pricing Page, the Choose Item Page, and the Custom Items Page.

Clicking the show/hide item cost button on any one of these pages automatically turns on/off the display on the other two pages as well.

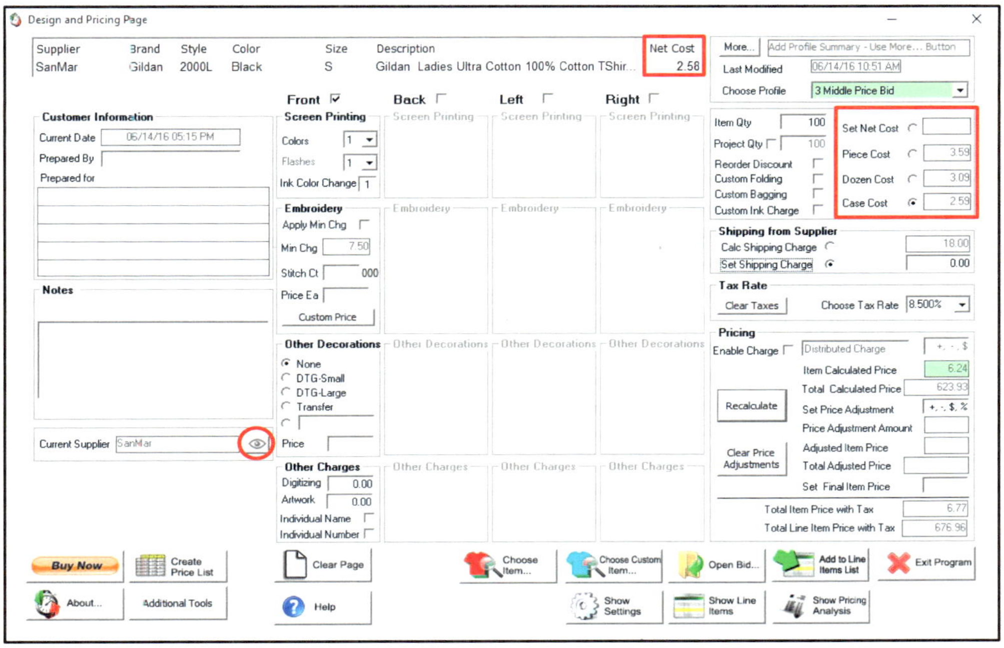

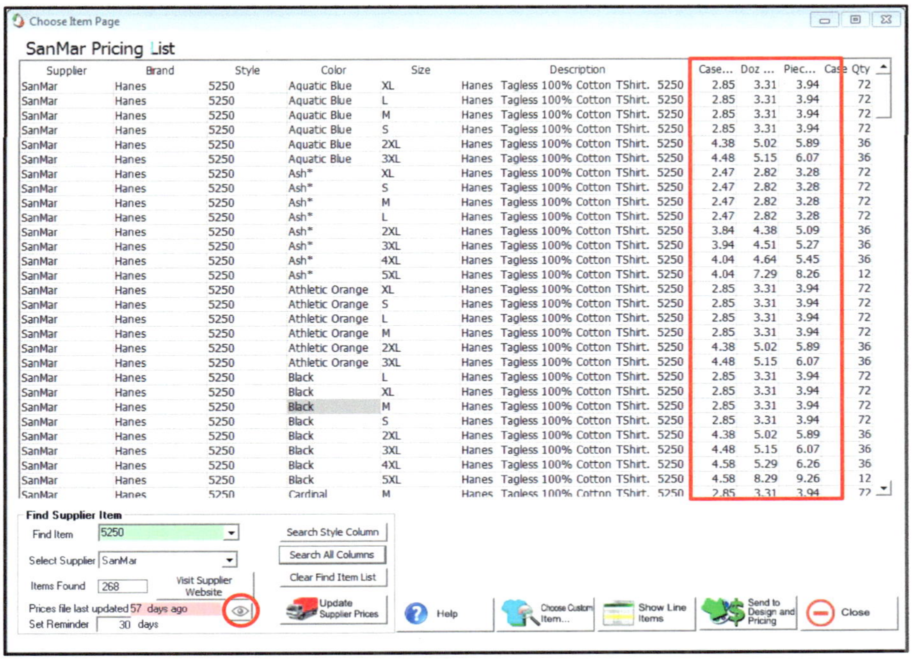

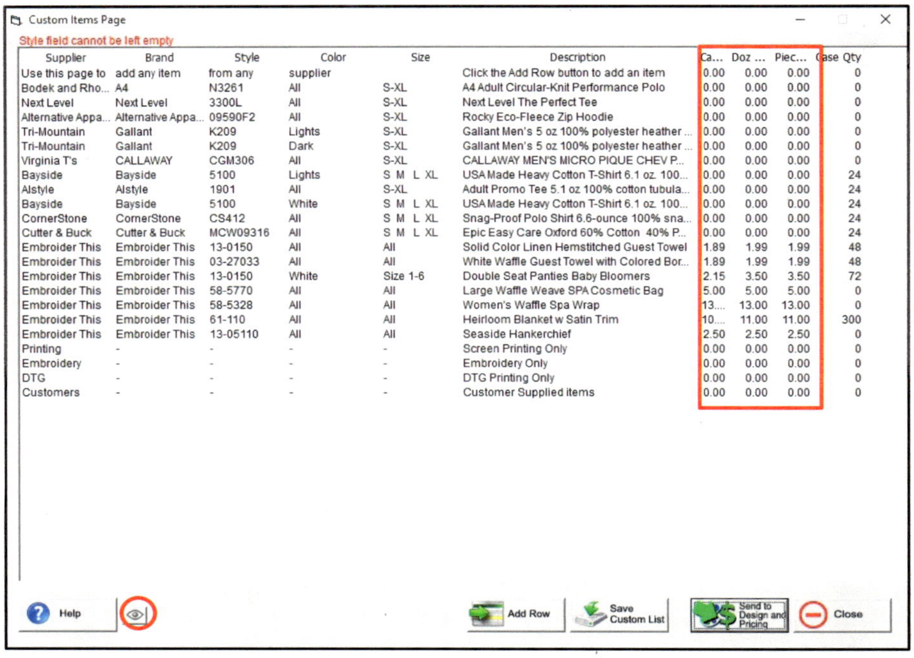

Things to Note:

- Unselecting **Show item cost** does not suppress the display of the net item cost on the Pricing Analysis Page.

Using the Pricing Analysis Page

The Pricing Analysis Page shows the contribution of each charge and discount to the final calculated price for the line item on your bid. It also shows general information such as the customer's name and contact information the sales person who prepared the bid, and the time and date the bid was created.

To access this page, click the **Show Pricing Analysis** button. The Pricing Analysis Page can be accessed from the Choose Item Page, Design and Pricing Page, and the Profile Settings Page. If you do not see the buttons, it means that a password has been set up for Fast Accurate Bids and you are using the program in User Mode. For more information see Using Password Protection.

In addition to using the Pricing Analysis Page to display the price information for the item currently on the Design and Pricing Page, you can use it to set a specific initial price and quantity and then see how various setting combinations on the Design and Pricing Page affect it.

Things to note

- If the window on the left of the Pricing Analysis Page is blank when you open it, it means that you have not yet added an item to the Design and Pricing Page.
- The **Set Item Cost** check box allows you to enter an initial price for a hypothetical item so you can see how each of the markup and discounts for the settings on the Design and Pricing Page affects the calculated price for the item. This feature provides a powerful tool for price analysis by starting with an easy to track amount and testing how various settings on the Design and Pricing Page, including switching from one pricing profile to another, affect the final calculated price.
- The **Item Qty** field allows you to enter a number of items for use in testing pricing analysis. The **Item Qty** field is intended to be used with **Set Item Cost**. For example, if you set **Set Item Cost** to $1.00 and **Number of Items** to 1, then you can clearly see how the settings on the Design and Pricing Page affect the final calculated price.
- Consider having both the Design and Pricing Page and the Pricing Analysis Page open side-by-side on your computer screen when doing pricing analysis, so you can see both pages at the same time.
- Selecting the **Summary** display shows only the general information about the line item and the charges and discounts that have been applied to the line item in the display.
- Selecting the **Detail** display shows the general information about the line item, and all possible options, charges, and discounts providing a zero for charges and discounts not applied to the line item in the display.

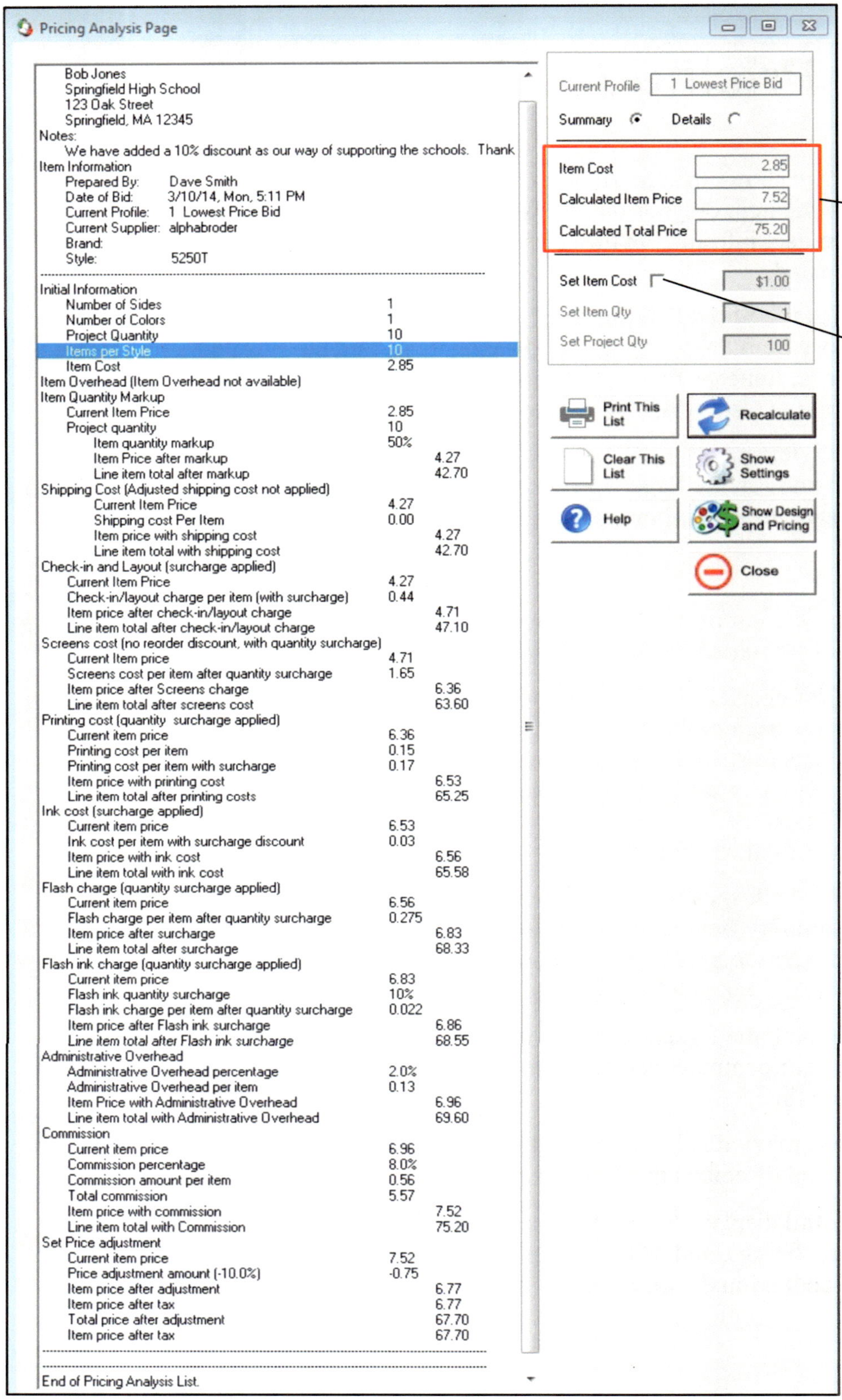

The values for the Item Cost, Calculated Item Price, and Calculated Total Price come from the current line item on the Design and Pricing Page.

Set Item Cost is a feature that allows you to do "what if" pricing analysis.

This check box lets you disregard the other price fields and specify the starting price and quantity.

- If you enter an amount in the **Set Final Price** field on the Design and Pricing Page, the Pricing Analysis Page still shows all the calculated amounts. In addition, it adds a section just below the general information to document that the price is a set price.
- If you don't see something in the pricing list that you think ought to be there, then check two things. If the item has a check box on the Design and Pricing Page, make sure that the check box is enabled and checked. If the item is listed in the settings list on the Profile Settings Page, be sure the price is not $0.00 and that the field is not blank.
- The Pricing Analysis Page provides a scroll bar for moving up and down the display window. You can also resize this page by hovering your mouse at the edge of the page and resizing it to be larger or smaller.
- If you click on a row in the main window of this page to highlight it and later want to get the highlight out of the way, click at the bottom of the page to park the highlight out of sight.
- Access to the Pricing Analysis Page can be hidden by turning on password protection for Fast Accurate Bids. For more information, see Using password protection.
- The **Print This List** button prints the information currently displayed in the window of the Pricing Analysis Page to your default printer. To print all of the information, especially when viewing the Detail view, you may need to print part of the information, scroll down the display and print the rest of it on a separate page.
- If you switch the default for your printers, for example, if you switch the default for your printer from your regular inkjet printer to a printer/plotter or a printer that you use for your sublimation work, make sure that the default is set to your regular printer before printing the Pricing Analysis Page.

Setting up price lists

Fast Accurate Bids offers a software extension called Price List Creator that lets you create screen printing price lists quickly and easily.

The Price List Creator Page lets you set up and configure price lists.

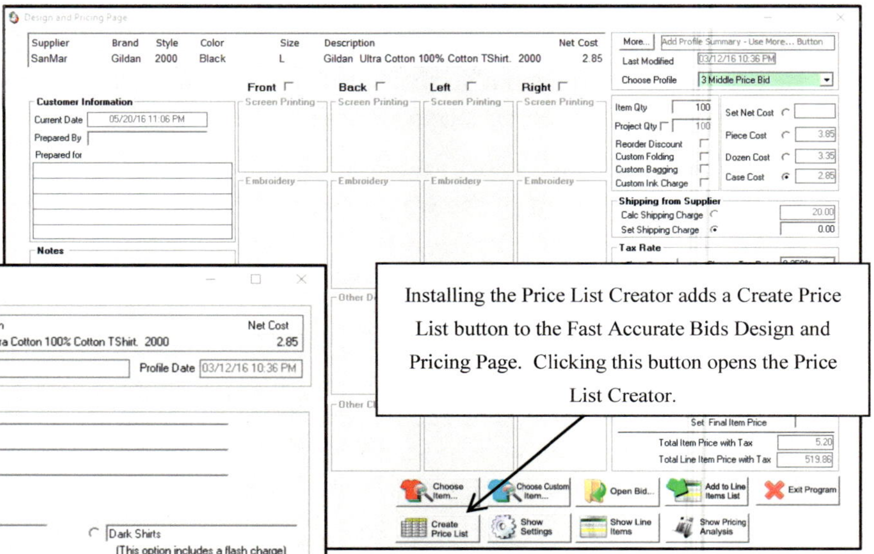

Installing the Price List Creator adds a Create Price List button to the Fast Accurate Bids Design and Pricing Page. Clicking this button opens the Price List Creator.

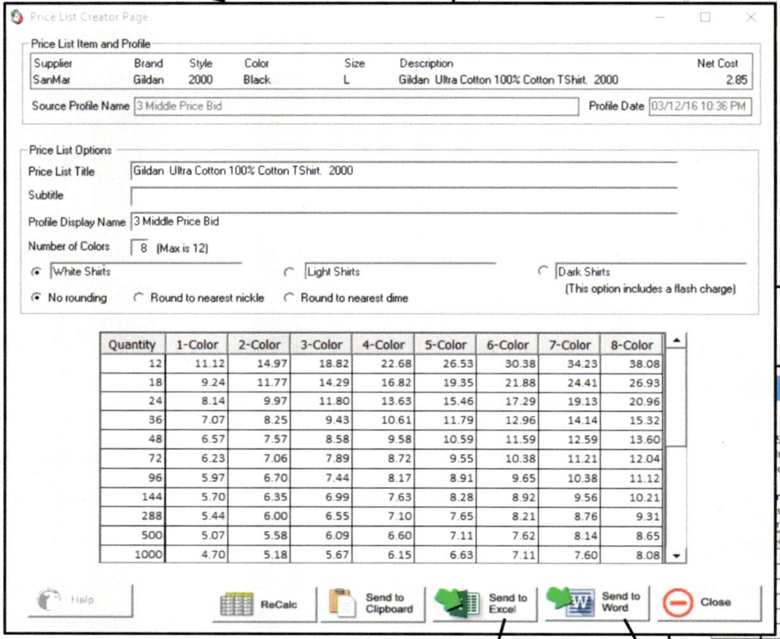

Quantity	1-Color	2-Color	3-Color	4-Color	5-Color	6-Color	7-Color	8-Color
12	11.12	14.97	18.82	22.68	26.53	30.38	34.23	38.08
18	9.24	11.77	14.29	16.82	19.35	21.88	24.41	26.93
24	8.14	9.97	11.80	13.63	15.46	17.29	19.13	20.96
36	7.07	8.25	9.43	10.61	11.79	12.96	14.14	15.32
48	6.57	7.57	8.58	9.58	10.59	11.59	12.59	13.60
72	6.23	7.06	7.89	8.72	9.55	10.38	11.21	12.04
96	5.97	6.70	7.44	8.17	8.91	9.65	10.38	11.12
144	5.70	6.35	6.99	7.63	8.28	8.92	9.56	10.21
288	5.44	6.00	6.55	7.10	7.65	8.21	8.76	9.31
500	5.07	5.58	6.09	6.60	7.11	7.62	8.14	8.65
1000	4.70	5.18	5.67	6.15	6.63	7.11	7.60	8.08

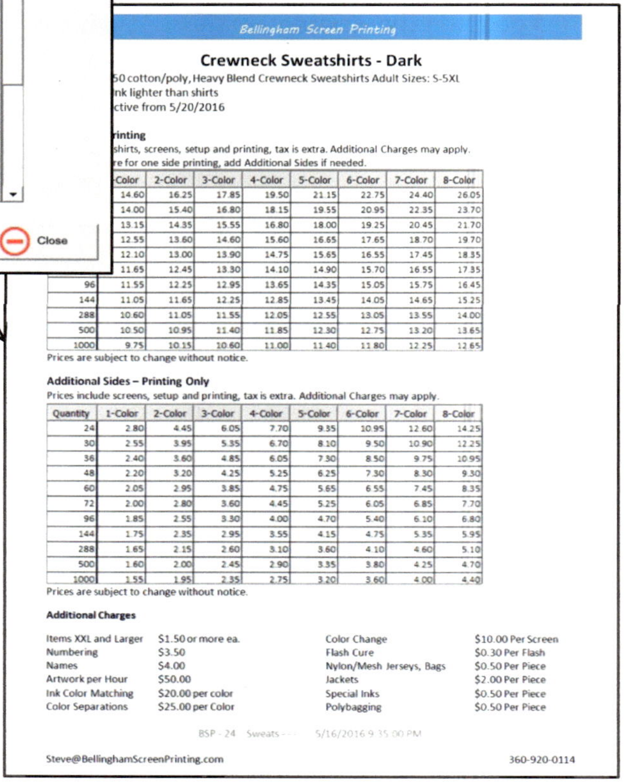

The finished price lists can be sent to a Microsoft Excel spreadsheet and a Microsoft Word file.

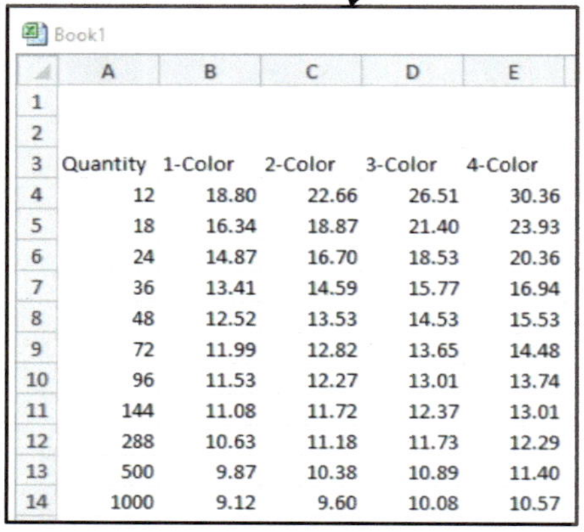

	A	B	C	D	E
1					
2					
3	Quantity	1-Color	2-Color	3-Color	4-Color
4	12	18.80	22.66	26.51	30.36
5	18	16.34	18.87	21.40	23.93
6	24	14.87	16.70	18.53	20.36
7	36	13.41	14.59	15.77	16.94
8	48	12.52	13.53	14.53	15.53
9	72	11.99	12.82	13.65	14.48
10	96	11.53	12.27	13.01	13.74
11	144	11.08	11.72	12.37	13.01
12	288	10.63	11.18	11.73	12.29
13	500	9.87	10.38	10.89	11.40
14	1000	9.12	9.60	10.08	10.57

Here's just a few ways that the Price List Creator can help you in your business:

- Create one or more price lists for your website.
- Create individual price lists for the sample apparel items in your showroom.
- Create sample price lists to insert into the apparel catalogs you send to prospects.
- Create sales price lists to send to your customers.
- Create contract printing price lists for the apparel decoration businesses you serve.
- Create price lists to assist you in developing and refining the settings for your Fast Accurate Bids custom pricing profiles.
- Create price lists to assist you in setting up pricing in other software programs such as Ink Soft, Deconet, and QuickBooks.

Price List Creator can only be used with a licensed version of Fast Accurate Bids (version 3.5.0 or later). It's available from the Fast Accurate Bids website.

For more information, see the Price List Creator Manual.

Glossary

Admin Overhead - is a field in the Overhead Charges area of the Profile Settings Page. This field sets the percentage to be charged to cover overhead costs such as your production margin, rent, non-billable staff time, equipment costs, utility bills, and insurance. When used, administrative overhead is calculated on the price of the item just prior to applying the commission percentage. (Admin Overhead is not applied on the net cost for items.)

Bid Files - are produced when you click **Save Bid** on the Line Items Page to save the current bid information to your Windows file system. Bid files always end with the file extension **.bid**.

Calculated Shipping - is the estimated cost of shipping the items from your supplier to your shop. It is calculated as the higher of either (Net Item Price x Items per Style x Wholesale Shipping Percent) or the amount specified on the Setting Page in the field Wholesale Min Shipping.

Check In/Layout - is a field in the Overhead Charges area of the Profile Settings Page. This field sets the charge per item that you want used to cover the time it takes to unpack items, count them, stack them for decoration, lay them out again after decoration, recount them, and repack them for delivery.

Custom Ink Charge/Color - is a field in the Screen Printing Charges area of the Profile Settings Page. This field sets the additional amount you charge for screen printing on items that require an additive for the ink. This charge is intended to recover the cost of ink that must be discarded after printing the job, for example printing on nylon items. The custom ink charge per color is multiplied by the sum of the **Screen Print** quantities and the **Item Qty** to determine the amount to charge.

Custom Item - is any item that you cannot select from the Choose Item Page because you do not have a supplier connector for the company from which you intend to order them. The Custom Item Page lets you set up and manage your list of custom items.

DTG - is also known as digital direct to garment printing, D2G printing, digital garment printing and inkjet to garment printing. It is a process of printing on textiles and garments using specialized or modified inkjet technology. DTG printers use specialty inks (inkjet textile inks) that are applied to the textile directly and are absorbed by the fibers.

Exclude Overhead Charges - is a check box that appears in the Name/Number Charges, Embroidery Charges, and Other Decoration Charges areas of the Profile Settings Page. These check boxes let you to specify whether you want the associated charges to be the exact amount to the customer or whether you want Fast Accurate Bids to calculate and add Check In/Layout, Admin Overhead, and Commission to these charges. Thus, if you have already factored in your handling, overhead, and commission on your embroidery other decoration and name and number charges, then selecting this check box lets you continue to use the amount for these charges that you are accustomed to using.

Flash Ink Surcharge - is a field in the Screen Printing Charges area of the Profile Settings Page. This field sets the markup percentage that is applied to the **Ink Charge/Color** field to calculate the ink charge for items that are flashed.

Flashing - is the process of using a heating unit on a screen printed garment while it is still on the press. The temperature of the ink layer on the garment is raised to the point where the ink begins to dry but is not completely cured. The ink will be dry to the touch and will form a solid surface on which to print additional colors. When the garment is run through the dryer the flashed layer will cure completely and bond to the ink layers on top.

Flashing Charge/Color - is a field in the Screen Printing Charges area of the Profile Settings Page. This field sets the additional amount you charge to cover the time it takes to flash cure ink during printing. There are fields on the Design and Pricing Page for selecting the number of flashes for each of the sides of the item.

Full Search - is one of the two options on the Update Prices dialog box. A Full Search enables the Fast Accurate Bids Supplier Connector to search your computer's full hard drive to locate the downloaded supplier pricing file. If you prefer to specify a directory for downloading the supplier pricing files that is other than the Windows Downloads directory, use this search option.

Ink Charge/Color - is a field in the Screen Printing Charges area of the Profile Settings Page. This field sets the amount you charge for ink to print one color on one item.

Ink Color Change - is a field in the Screen Printing area of the Design and Pricing Page. This field lets you add a charge if the job requires changing the ink color for one or more screens. This charge is intended to cover the time it takes to clean the ink from a screen and re-ink it. The amount that gets charged is determined by the amount in the field **Ink Color Change** on the Profile Settings Page.

Item Cost - is a field on the Design and Pricing page. This is the amount that you pay to your supplier for the items you sell. When you enter an item by selecting it from the Choose Item Page, the item cost is taken from the data in the supplier's pricing file. When you enter an item using the Custom Item Page, the item cost in the **Item Cost** field is taken from the data from that page.

Item Overhead is a field in the Item Charges area of the Profile Settings Page. This field sets the percentage to be charged to cover costs such as misprints, defective items, time for ordering items, etc. When used, item overhead is applied to the item cost of the items sold.

Item Qty - is a field on the Design and Pricing page that lets you enter the quantity for a particular line item. See also Project Qty.

Itemized Bids - show the pricing for each of the components of an apparel decoration job as opposed to standard bids and mixed item bids which show inclusive pricing. For example, an itemized bid for embroidery might show the price for the undecorated garment, the digitizing, and the embroidery. Itemized bids often show both a total price per item and total price for the job.

Mixed Item Bid – is a bid that presents an assortment of items that will receive the same decoration. For example, a mixed item bid might offer the pricing for placing the same image on 100 T-Shirts, 25 sweatshirts, and 25 hoodies. Mixed item bids show the price per item and can optionally have a totals row as well to show the total number of items and the total price for the job.

Name - is a field in the Name/Number Charges area of the Profile Settings Page. This field sets the amount you charge for putting individual names (or any individual words) on shirts. For example, putting individual employees' names and their job titles on shirts. The charge for Name gets applied when you select the check box for **Individual Name** on the Design and Pricing Page.

Owner Mode- when you set up a password in Fast Accurate Bids, you are actually setting the ability for the software to run in either Owner mode or User mode. Owner mode means that the Choose Item, Design and Pricing, and Line Items pages provide buttons to access the Profile Settings Page and the Pricing Analysis Page. The program can be started in Owner mode by entering the correct password in the field **Enter Password** on the Design and Pricing Page. If no password is set, the program operates in the same manner as it does in Owner mode.

Price List Creator - is a Fast Accurate Bids software extension that lets you create screen printing price lists quickly and easily.

.

Pricing Profile - is a list of the charges, markups, discounts, and other settings that are used as the variable values for this program that has been saved under a descriptive name so that you can select it for use when creating bids. This information includes all the settings and values on the Fast Accurate Bids Profile Settings Page, all the settings and values on the Program Preferences dialog box, and two settings on the Design and Pricing page, specifically the name in the Prepared By field, and the setting for the check box related to showing the customer name on the bid. Pricing profiles end with the file suffix **.pro**.

Printing Charge/Color - is a field in the Screen Printing Charges area of the Profile Settings Page. This field sets the amount you charge for labor to print one color on one item.

Project Qty - is the total of all items for the bid if customer wants the same decoration on different types of items. See also Item Qty.

Quick Search - is one of the two options on the Update Prices dialog box. A Quick Search limits searching for a downloaded supplier pricing file to just your Windows downloads folder. This option can be used to significantly speed up the process for updating the supplier prices if you allow the pricing file to be downloaded to your Windows Downloads directory.

Screen Charge/Color - is a field in the Screen Printing Charges area of the Profile Settings Page. This field is for the amount you charge the customer for each screen for printing. It is intended to cover the labor and materials associated with the use of the screen.

The labor portion consists of the cost of coating the screen, burning the image on it, taping it for printing, registering it on the press, and after the job is done, reclaiming it for future work.

The materials portion consists of a percentage of the cost screen itself (which is based on the number of times the screen can be used), the emulsion for the screen, the film for the image, the tape, and the chemicals.

Standard Bids - present an assortment of choices so the customer can choose one. For example, a standard bid might offer a choice of quantities (24, 36, 48), or a choice of garments (for example, good, better, best) to allow the customer to select the one that is the best match for he wants. Standard bids show the price per item and don't provide a totals row since the underlying assumption is that the customer will only select one of the options offered by the bid.

Supplier Connector - is the generic name for the programs Fast Accurate Bids provides for downloading and working with the electronic supplier pricing files available from wholesale apparel companies. Fast Accurate Bids includes one supplier connector of your choice when you download the software. You may also purchase additional supplier connectors at that time or later whenever you want.

User Mode - when you set up a password in Fast Accurate Bids, you are actually setting the ability for the software to run in either Owner mode or User mode. User mode means that the **Show Settings** and **Pricing Analysis** buttons will not appear on the Design and Pricing, Choose Item, and Line Items pages. This means that unless the user is aware of using the program in Owner mode, he or she will not even know that these pages exist.

Index

T

U

W

Made in United States
Troutdale, OR
11/03/2026

56844696R00040